Transforming

Rob and Nick Carter

Transforming

The Fine Art Society Contemporary   2013

for **Jo**

Rob and Nick Carter
Transforming for 15 Years
Kate Bryan   6

Archive   1998–2012

Transforming   2013

Rob and Nick Carter
Transforming for 15 Years

RN160 **Self Portrait**   2002
framed fibre-based print
24 × 24 in   61 × 61 cm
edition of 12

Rob and Nick Carter are not interested in making artwork that looks like a 'Rob and Nick Carter'. Nor are they keen to be identified by working with a particular medium. For the past 15 years they have resisted simple categorisation by consistently creating new departures in their practice. In exploring various media they continually push the boundaries between painting, sculpture, installation, neon, digital imagery and photography, often creating works which cannot be defined in one sense alone. This multi-faceted and democratic approach to media does not result in a lack of consistency — it is certainly there, manifested in a myriad of subtle, evolving and interconnected ways. This volume is dedicated to their relentless creativity and presents the journey of their artistic partnership since the late nineties.

The genesis of their working relationship was in the simple act of Nick painting upon Rob's photographs and, *vice versa*, Rob photographing Nick's paintings. From the outset they were transgressing the boundaries between traditional art mediums and interrogating analogue and digital modes of working. In the earliest series, **Grid Pictures**[16] (2000) and **Painting Photographs**[106] (2005) the collision of their

independent scholarship of art history and painting (Nick at Goldsmiths) and fine art photography (Rob) is evident. They provide possibly the only instance in their artistic output when the viewer is able to discern what is 'Rob' and what is 'Nick'. Afterwards their involvement became seamless and neither will ever be drawn on what they each contribute to a particular series or artwork. It is not so much secrecy on their part as much as probably not even knowing themselves — the result of a profoundly interconnected partnership.

Grid Pictures (2000) introduced the grid presentation that would become a recurrent feature in their practice. The graphic quality of the boldly coloured photographic series belies the 'handmade' quality of creation — light-sensitive paper is set to spin on a potter's wheel and small amounts of paint added after the exposure creates organic splashes at odds with the geometric grid formation. **Painting Photographs** (2005) were created by taking macro photographs of lush, thick paintbrush marks. The artists were interested in the notion that even exquisite masterpieces in the National Gallery were abstract when you looked closely — the paint was full of its own strong forms independent of the composition. The original paintings executed in a

miniature format on glass were destroyed so all that remained was the photographic record, presented in a frame that better suited an oil painting. It was an idea that would come to define the Carters – simple, focused and immaculately presented. Their debut works carry many features that would come to be signatures of their practice – creating a hybrid between two modes of making art; acknowledging colour, form and light as central to the image and creating a tension between analogue and digital.

The next few years were defined by working in the dark producing multiple series that explored cameraless photography and the possibilities of 'light paintings'. These works were made against a backdrop of dramatic changes in the photographic market. Access to powerful cameras became straightforward and the practice of digitally manipulating images ubiquitous. Series such as **Spectrum Circles**[22], **Vertical Lines**[28], **Coloured Light Projections**[36], **Light Paintings**[40], **Multi-coloured Lines**[46], **Colour Spirals**[52], **Mag Lights**[70] and **Harmonographs**[76] circumnavigate traditional photographic technique and resist the normal parameters of the medium. The works are made without the use of a camera or a lens; the Carters employ a

myriad of light sources with which to 'paint with light' onto light-sensitive paper called Cibachrome. Although each series has its own point of difference in the way the various instruments of light are produced and captured, at the heart of the various Cibachrome series is an exploration of colour, light and form.

In one of these light painting series the artists employed neon as a light source (**Neon Landscapes**[64] [2004]) and ultimately the Carters came to have a more sustained relationship with the medium, promoting it to be the finished artwork rather than a tool in a Cibachrome work. The vibrant **Postcards from Vegas**[154] series (2010) unites neon and photography to create sculptural wall based works. Each artwork is a product of various appropriations and consists of a blown-up reproduction of a vintage postcard (complete with evidence of the original card's wear and tear) overlaid with a remade neon sign from Vegas. The artworks marry deliberately opposing imagery to create an impactful juxtaposition, one that is both bold and charmingly nostalgic. The series deploys clashing art historical styles such as picturesque with pop. However, closer inspection reveals that each combination coheres in a subtle fashion and avoids disjuncture with careful mirroring and visual echoes. The results are surprising; far from jarring the neon series speak of the pre-digital era whilst simultaneously presenting a highly original and contemporary aesthetic.

Several of their neon works came to be fashioned as large-scale permanent installations such as **Revolution in Two Parts**[86] (2010) at Aldersgate opposite the Museum of London, **Wavelength**[84] (2006) in Victoria and **Wavelength Through Blue**[92] (2009) in Savile Row. The works in neon are not just a development in medium, they also marked an interesting departure into movement. Each utilises the possibility of programming the work to change, either revolving through colour spectrums or activating moving neon light by nearby movement, thus presenting the viewer with a constantly evolving visual experience.

It has long been written that Rob and Nick Carter's work is centered on the possibilities of colour, light and form. This was certainly true and integral to their earliest series and remains important. However, what has emerged is a larger, over-reaching concern that has propelled their artwork forward into new and even more engaging territory. That is the notion of perception and how we engage with and see a work of art. They underscore this by examining how they might deliver visual transformations in their practice to better emphasise the viewer's position in the dynamic between the artwork and its reception.

This was succinctly embodied with another neon series, **Read Colours Not Words**[96] (2009) that was installed on Islington High Street. It is formed of six rows of seven words. Each was made of neon and spelled a different colour such as RED or BLUE, but each was created with a colour of neon at odds with the word. For instance the letters that spelt ORANGE might glow in bright blue neon. Here, as with all of their work, the Carters put colour (not words) first. **Public Perception of Colour**[128] (2009) continued with the theme of how we read colour and marked their first foray into public participation. The viewer was invited to select a Pantone colour sample that they felt best represented a word such as 'red'. The diverse results could not be predicted and serve as a compelling exploration into how radically different our understanding of colour can be.

The Carters have always allowed room for a level of unpredictability in their practice – the failure rate of many of the light paintings was incredibly high, especially for the intricate **Spectrum Circles** series made using fine light sources and a spinning potter's wheel. Chance became a more seriously incorporated component in two series made outside of the studio and both involving paint in 2012, **Unconscious Paintings**[114] and **Paint Pigment Photographs**[132]. **Unconscious Paintings** are entirely dependent on chance as the majority of the creative act happens completely outside of the artists' hands. The experimental series is a development of the surrealist notion of unconscious painting. Small bottles of paint lean precariously over the edges of a clean canvas prepared by the Carters. The paint does not unleash its potential until after the piece is sent via Royal Mail, encased in a Perspex box and hidden in a shipping crate. Each work is formed of one colour and is sent with instructions to an international museum with the objective being that it is returned to sender. Exposed to random, incalculable activity, the concept subverts the traditional relationship between artist and artwork, the artwork and museum and the limits between paint, canvas and sculpture.

Paint Pigment Photographs neatly demonstrate the artists' preoccupation with light, colour and form and the series is underscored by chance and unpredictability. The Hindu festival of *Holi* inspired the action photography that captures paint pigment spontaneously thrown into the air. Explosions of coloured pigment captured at 1/8000th of a second retain the energy of the act itself, suspended in space. The resulting photograph, no easy thing to create, is a physical manifestation of the actual performance, creating an imprint of the spontaneous and unrepeatable gesture. The series plays on the transient nature of light and form, and also creates a dialogue about the ephemeral aspect of art. The genesis of the series is in the transformative act of throwing the pigment – turning a static painting ingredient into an active gesture and recording a split second of its time suspended against the clouds.

The 2013 exhibition for which this book has been compiled, presents a new body of work that has been over three years in the making with the notion of transforming at its core. However, the theme of transformation has been a subtle but guiding force in many of their artworks, not only **Paint Pigment Photographs** but also in the act of appropriation in **Postcards From Vegas**, the revolving neon circles and the colour changing lights used in their exhibition at the Museum of Neon Art in Los Angeles. Even the Carters' early series, **Painting Photographs**, was dependent on the concept of transformation – from making something figurative become abstract and in the manipulation of boundaries between what is created by the artists and what is seen by the viewer. In their hands imagery is often in a state of transformation, from one medium to another and this heightens our visual appetite, presenting more than one way of looking and understanding.

The critical point of genesis for the exhibition **Transforming** was created between 2009 and 2012. **Transforming Still Life Painting**[178] takes as its subject a Dutch Golden Age masterpiece by Ambrosius Bosschaert the Elder. Working with MPC, the Carters created an animated version of Bosschaert's **Vase With Flowers in a Window**. Every aspect has been brought to life and the seamless three-hour loop takes the painted scene from dusk to dawn. Only perceptible upon sustained looking, the still life displays subtle shifts as the clouds pass by, the sun moves in the sky and the stars emerge. Each flower has been informed by actual time-lapse footage of real flowers throughout the course of the day, marking subtle shifts in bloom and direction as they turn to face the sun. Every few minutes the still life displays real-time activity, such as a caterpillar eating leaves. In their homage the artists examine the boundaries between the real and the imagined, analogue and digital, and the traditional and the progressive.

Their world first 'digital painting' provided a unique intersection between the worlds of Old Master connoisseurship and the dynamic world of contemporary new media art. It was selected by *The Art Newspaper* as a top five pick at TEFAF; an Old Master dealer who acquired an edition described it as "better than the real thing" in *The New York Times* and Sir Peter Blake, the eminent pop artist and avid collector, described it as the most important addition to his collection in the past decade. Despite its accolades (it is on permanent display at the Manchester Museum of Art; it will be on display at New York's

Frick Collection from October 2013 to January 2014 and has been accepted into the Mauritshuis permanent collection) it has not yet been part of a Rob and Nick Carter exhibition and will be an important anchor for the show.

Joining it will be three new time-based media works made with MPC that adopt an Old Master painting in a groundbreaking form of homage. **Transforming Vanitas Painting**[190] (2013) is based on the 1630 oil on copper **Dead Frog with Flies** by Ambrosius Bosschaert the Younger. In the three-hour sequence the Carters underscore the sensitive presentation of *vanitas* by taking the scene from the last few minutes of the creature's life through various stages of decay and ultimate decomposition. The genius of the Carters' vision is that it captures the decaying frog, but the viewer is always conscious that visually this is very much a painted frog. Every brushstroke and texture is captured and the entire scene treated not as a biological survey into decomposition, but as a moving, 'living' painting. This is *vanitas* painting for the twenty-first century.

Transforming Diptych[202] (2013) brings to life a pair of still life paintings by Justus Juncker dating from 1765. The Carters have drawn inspiration from the monumental and mysterious presentation of the fruits by Juncker. Their work ostensibly appears to be two independently framed, quiet paintings. Sustained looking reveals that not only have the Carters brought the scenes alive, they have created a deep interconnection. As a butterfly leaves one frame, it disappears into the space of gallery wall and reappears moments later on the other fruit. In line with their previous interest in chance and unpredictability, the Carters have directed MPC to develop sophisticated programming that results in a cycle of activity unlikely to be predicted or seen in exactly the same order.

The artists have also taken on the challenge of Giorgione's **Sleeping Venus** in **Transforming Nude Painting**[212] (2013). The Carters have breathed life into the masterpiece, transporting the viewer to the Venetian landscape where Venus peacefully sleeps as the day passes. In a similar vein to the gentle passage of time in **Transforming Still Life Painting**, the scene passes from dawn to dusk imperceptibly. This is a deeply evocative, highly naturalistic presentation

REC

Dur 01:34:03:12

of a goddess sleeping. Venus' chest rises and falls, occasionally her foot twitches or her hand stirs. Giorgione's original painting was a careful balancing act between a scene of idyllic rural contemplation and a sensual presentation of a beautiful nude. The Carters have heightened this paradox by creating a serene depiction of passing time that displays tantalising moments of eroticism as Venus unconsciously moves her fingers across her body. Presented on a 4K screen, the piece marks a huge development in the employment of digital rendering and sculpting, blending actual footage of a sleeping model with digitally generated imagery.

The Carters were partly motivated to create these works upon learning that the average time we spend looking at an artwork in a museum or gallery is six seconds. These time-based media works encourage us to look again and reward sustained engagement, bringing a remote historical period back into focus. Crucially, the Carters resist the temptation to take the selected artworks into the realm of science fiction and instead use the arsenal of digital techniques at their disposal to underscore the brilliance and poignancy of the original paintings.

To the same end but via different means, the Carters have created their first two works of sculpture. The artists worked with MPC to turn paintings into completely three-dimensional digital files. These files are then given form using 3D printing which provides the basis for a lost wax bronze – allowing for a level of detail and delicacy not possible even two years ago. **Sunflowers232** (2013) bestows an entirely new sculptural form to Vincent van Gogh's celebrated post-impressionist masterpiece from 1888 in the collection of London's National Gallery. The quality of the 3D rendering and printing is the most advanced in the world and combined they offer a minutely detailed replica of the original artwork from all angles. Cast using the lost wax process, the finished sculpture is one of the most complex and detailed bronzes ever produced.

Created in the same fashion, **Black Tulip224** (2012) is based on a watercolour of an 'Early Brabantsson' tulip by Judith Leyster dating from 1643. There is a quietness and subtle beauty to the Carters' sculptural rendition. It stands for more than twenty-first-century digital triumph – rather it takes the viewer full circle to marvel at Dutch Golden Age realism and allows us to share in that culture's delight of an exotic and sculptural flower.

The exhibition also includes various works of a photographic nature that transform paintings from various moments in art history. **Pixelated Paintings**[242] (2013) is a development of earlier work dealing with perception and how we 'read' a work of art. The artists enquire as to whether there are some paintings that are so deeply embedded in our cultural psyche that we know them even if they are reduced to a highly pixelated image. The change that these masterpieces — from Van Gogh to Leonardo to Munch — have undergone also implores the viewer to look again, this time with fresh eyes. The series also demonstrates the essential truth of all paintings — realist or abstract — that they are artifices (much like the **Painting Photographs**). The Carters make us see that every iconic work of art is just that — a work of art, a fabrication of someone else's making, a pictorial illusion that overtime we have learnt to 'read'.

The notion of perception is crucial to the series **Chinese Whispers**[266]. The Carters selected various Warhol drawings and paintings which they then requested be copied by hand in enormous workshops in southern China. The finished copy was forwarded to a second unsuspecting artisan to again be copied. This went on many times over, in the form of an artistic Chinese whisper. The mistakes and variations made by each artist were adopted and built upon by the next, completely transforming the original. The Carters have brought together each individual work to form large sequential collections that are completely unique. The artisans involved have no knowledge of their collective enterprise and the Carters have almost no control over the finished product — for once they are able to revel in mistakes rather than be victim to chance. In an entirely different manner to the digital paintings, this witty series insists upon close inspection and also draws attention to larger issues relating to image perception in the East and West and authenticity in art.

Also making use of the Chinese copyists is the **Composite Portraits**[300] series. In each artwork the Carters present an amalgamation of various paintings by an important artist such as Rembrandt. Taking photofit principles as their aesthetic benchmark, the artists use digital manipulation to create a new composite portrait from 'slices' of various head paintings by the artist. The digital image is discarded once it has been painted by hand in China; in the same way the paintings of their **Painting Photographs** were destroyed once they had been captured mechanically.

After 15 years the Carters have subverted their first ever series; here, analogue triumphs.

There are several photographically-based series in the exhibition such as **Dutch Flowers**[252], **Flowers in a Wan-Li Vase**[260] and **Six Portraits in Six Colours**[296], that transform an existing moment in art history with digital manipulation and presentation in analogue format on Cibachrome. It is fascinating to witness the various dialogues the artistic duo have created with analogue and digital technology over their career – at times taking an evangelical approach to sidelined practices such as **Photograms**[142] and now rather famously being pioneers in 'digital paintings'.

Transforming marks a milestone in the Carters' career. This large exhibition coincides with the 15-year anniversary of working together and marks a critical moment of sustained museum and institution interest in their work. But it also allows us enough distance to fully appreciate the interconnectedness of their multi-faceted and continually evolving artistic partnership. Visually distinct artworks such as **Postcards From Vegas**, **Spectrum Circles** and **Transforming Vanitas Painting** are certainly diverse in media but they emerge from a focused line of enquiry into perception and the transformative potential of images, both abstract and figurative.

The duration of their artistic partnership to date has been set against a backdrop of digital revolution and they have both resisted it and taken advantage of it – as testified to in the **Archive** section of this book. The **Transforming** exhibition presents a new body of work that re-engages with art of the past, harnessing the most cutting-edge new media to create a sustained engagement with old and modern masters. At the heart of the exhibition is a conviction that the rampant technological developments in our midst can be subverted from a tendency toward soulless image overload. Instead the Carters exploit all that is dynamic and groundbreaking in the digital age to facilitate a return to the art of sustained and deep looking. Whether abstract or figurative, the Carters deliver art that is immediate, immaculately polished and that – sometimes unexpectedly – greedily demands greater attention.

Kate Bryan
Head of Contemporary   The Fine Art Society
July 2013

Archive

Grid Pictures

RN113 **Mr Happy Reveller**   2000
unique Cibachrome prints with paint mounted on paper over board and framed
72 × 72 in   183 × 183 cm

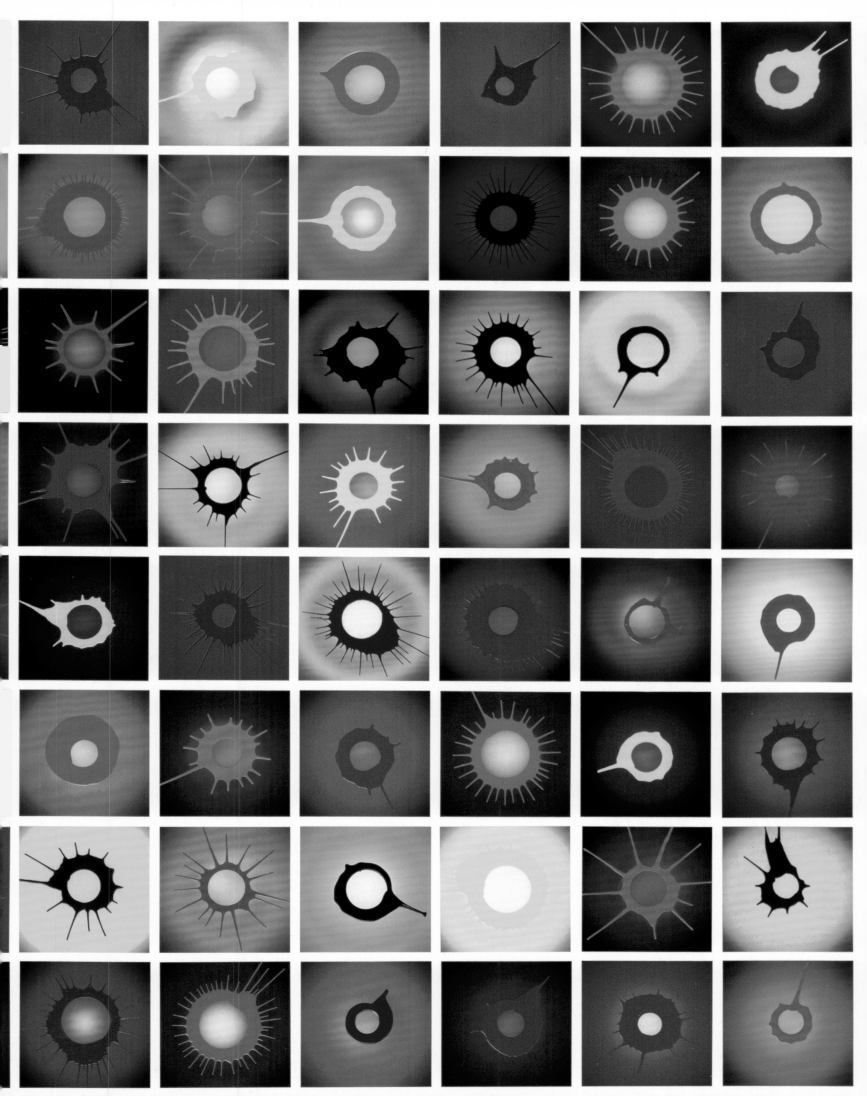

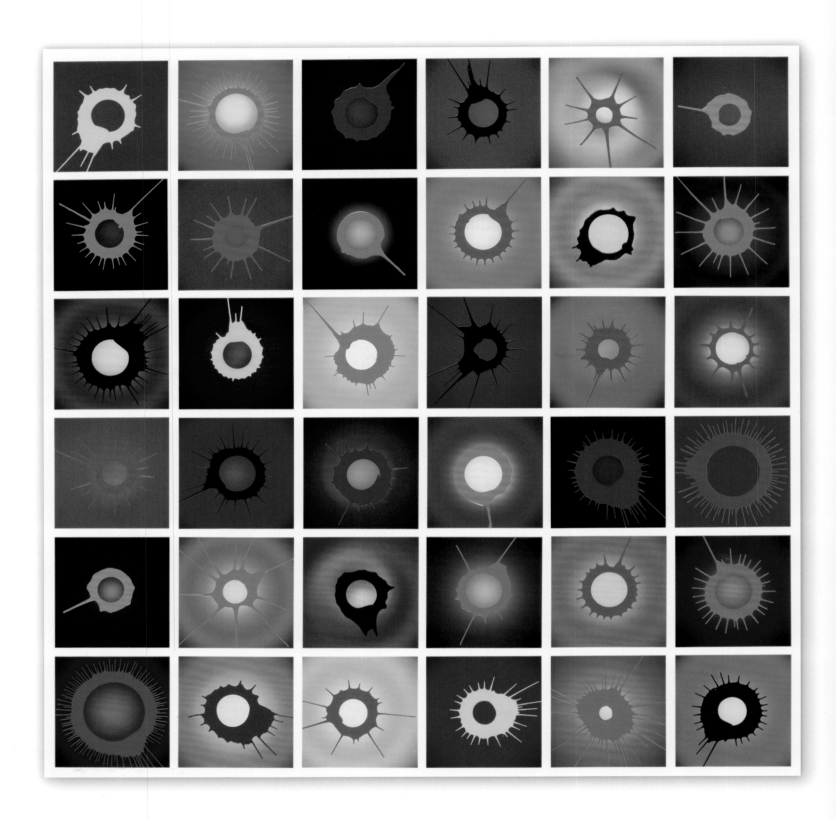

RN74 **Good Times** 2000
unique Cibachrome prints with paint mounted on paper over board and framed
55 × 55 in   140 × 140 cm

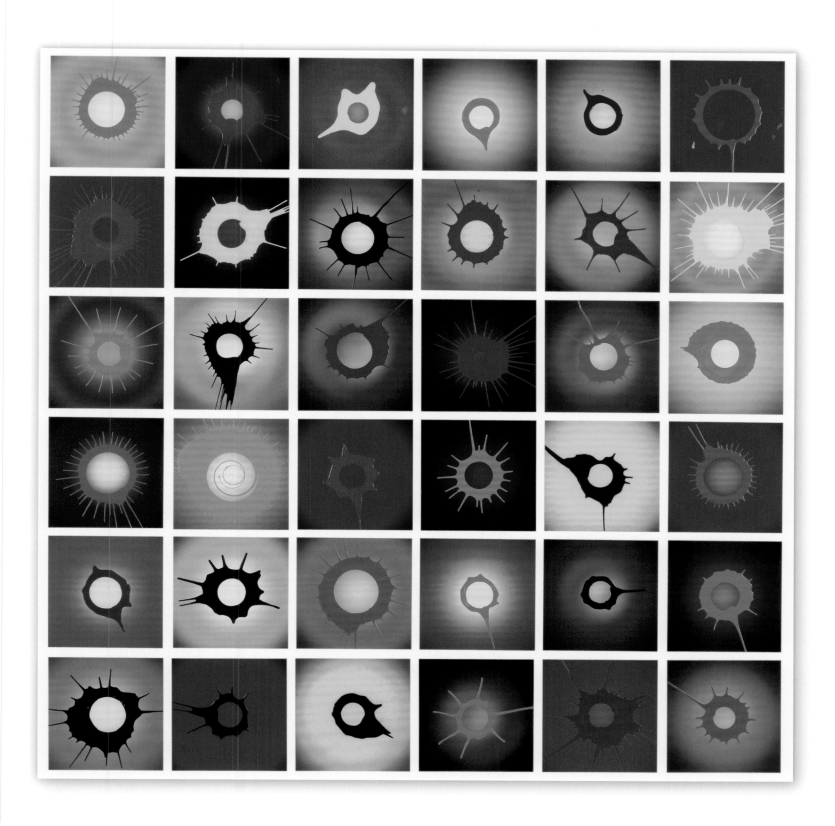

RN27 **Super Jackpot** 2000
unique Cibachrome prints with paint mounted on paper over board and framed
55 × 55 in   140 × 140 cm

RN64 **De Orbit** 2000
unique Cibachrome with paint mounted on aluminium and framed
44½ × 44½ in 113 × 113 cm

RN47 **Pressure Drop** 2000
unique Cibachrome with paint mounted on aluminium and framed
45 × 45 in   114 × 114 cm

The fun, variation, imagination, delight and wit that marks out Rob and Nick Carter's work are amongst the highlights of the British art world. Always refreshing and reinventing themselves, their pieces in so many media are often entertaining, always meticulous, exacting in their making and full of colour, surprise and detail. I am proud to be a Rob and Nick Carter addict.

Stephen Fry   Actor   Writer

Spectrum Circles

RN449 **Full Spectrum from Magenta to Purple**   2004
unique Cibachrome mounted on aluminium
41 × 41 in   104 × 104 cm

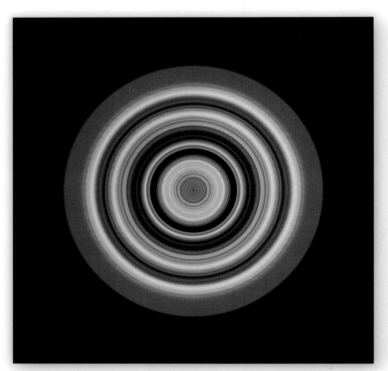

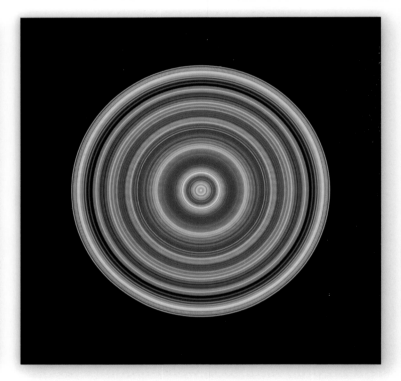

RN723 **Small Spectrum Circle** 2008
unique Cibachrome mounted on aluminium and framed
18 × 18 in   46 × 46 cm

RN724 **Small Spectrum Circle** 2008
unique Cibachrome mounted on aluminium and framed
18 × 18 in   46 × 46 cm

RN507 **Small Spectrum Circle** 2004
unique Cibachrome mounted on aluminium and framed
20 × 20 in   51 × 51 cm

RN722 **Small Spectrum Circle** 2008
unique Cibachrome mounted on aluminium and framed
18 × 18 in   46 × 46 cm

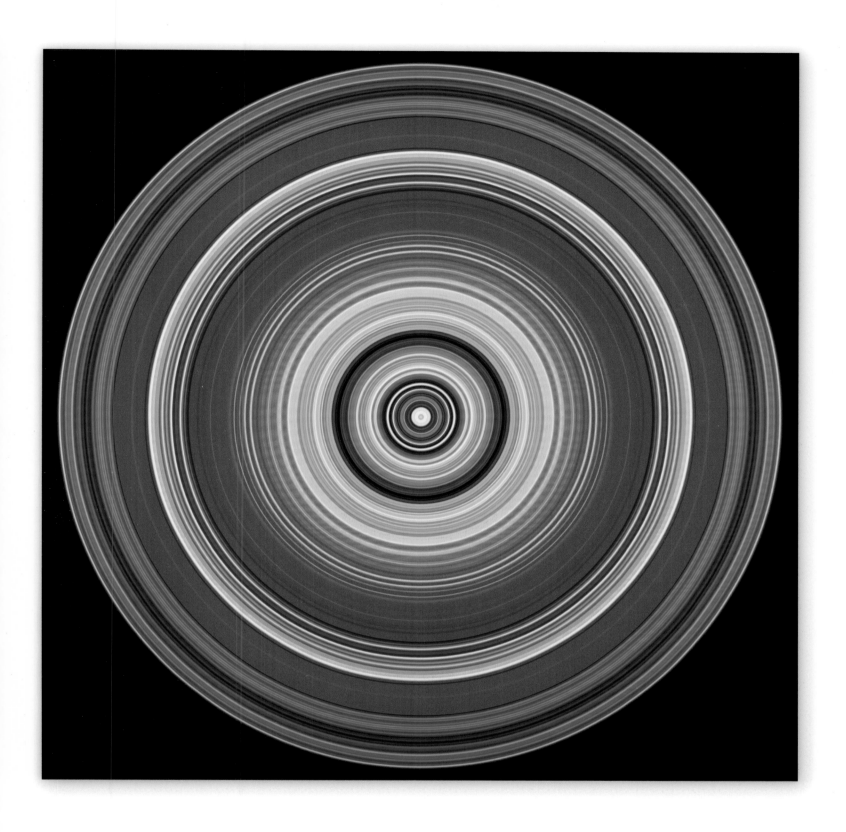

RN801 **Spectrum Circle** 2011
unique Cibachrome mounted on aluminium and framed
49 × 49 in 124 × 124 cm

Pulse State   2000
unique Cibachrome with paint mounted on aluminium and framed
46 × 46 in   117 × 117 cm

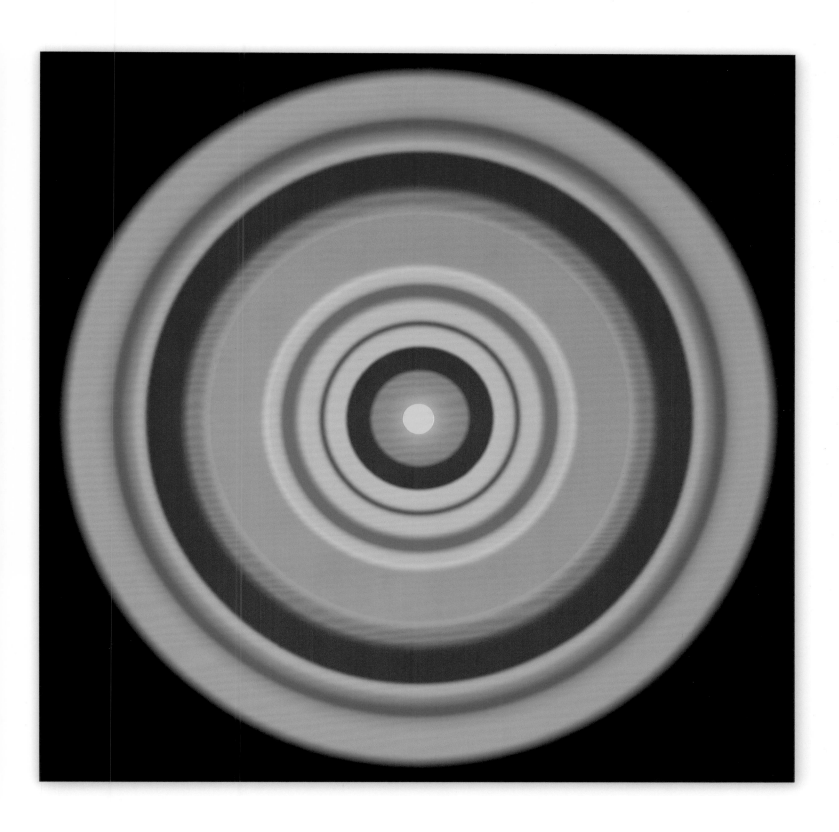

RN148 **Focus** 2001
unique Cibachrome with paint mounted on aluminium and framed
44 × 44 in   112 × 112 cm

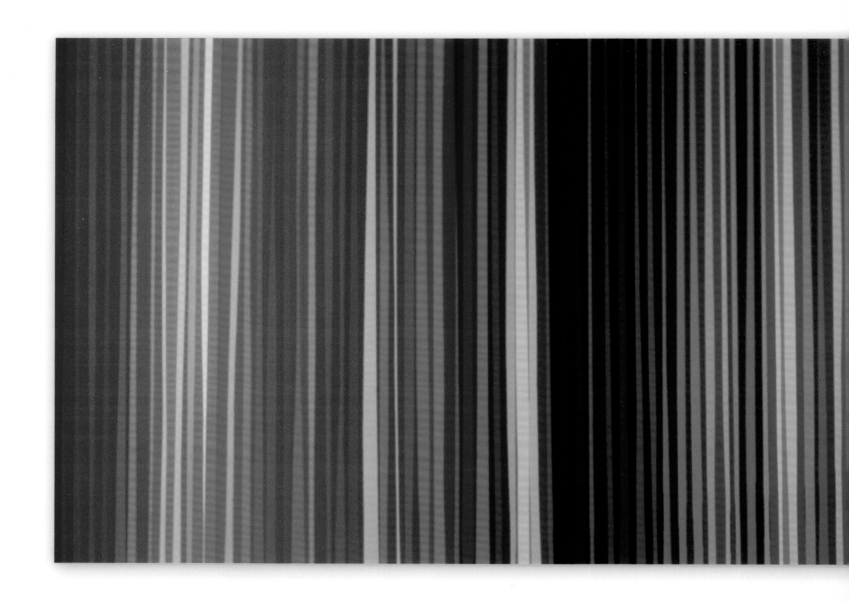

Vertical Lines

RN709 **Spectrum** 2008
unique Cibachrome mounted on aluminium and framed
96 × 35 in   244 × 89 cm

There are artists whose work is technically brilliant but no fun to look at. There are artists of whom the reverse is true. What a joy to see the work of Rob and Nick Carter, which is both clever and beautiful. In the years that I have known the couple I have admired and lusted after pieces from each evolution. I am enormously proud to own one of their light paintings from around 2004; its simplicity and serenity calm me every day as I barrel past it each morning on my way to work. I am also in awe of the enduring creative collaboration between Rob and Nick – most married couples I know would have garrotted each other with a fibre optic cable years ago, but these two manage to keep making amazing art together.

Lisa Markwell   Editor   *The Independent on Sunday*

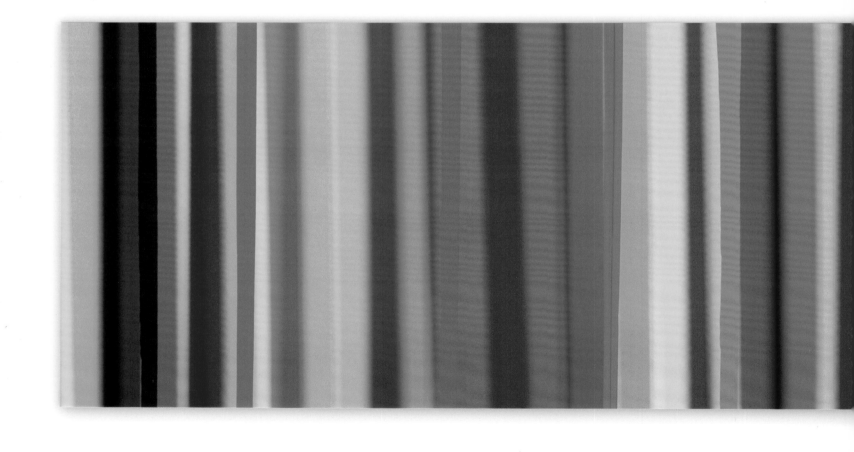

RN357 **Vertical Lines, Light and Paint**   2004
unique Cibachrome with paint mounted on aluminium and framed
38 × 12 in   97 × 30 cm

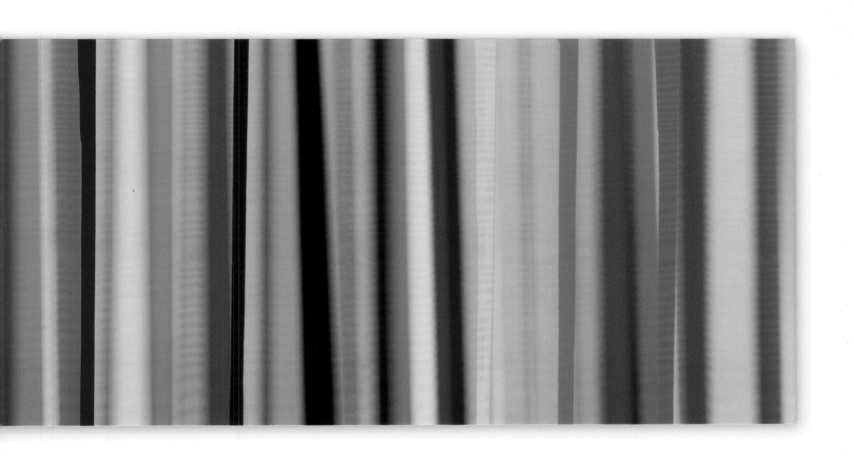

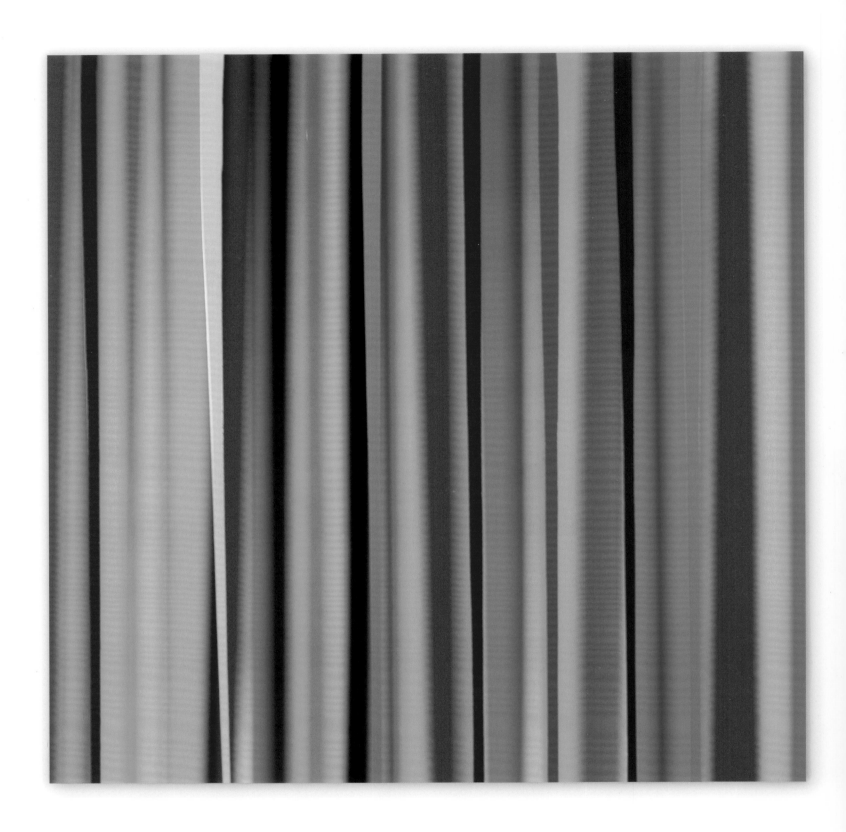

RN352 **Vertical Lines, Light and Paint**   2004
unique Cibachrome with paint mounted on aluminium and framed
24 × 24 in   61 × 61 cm

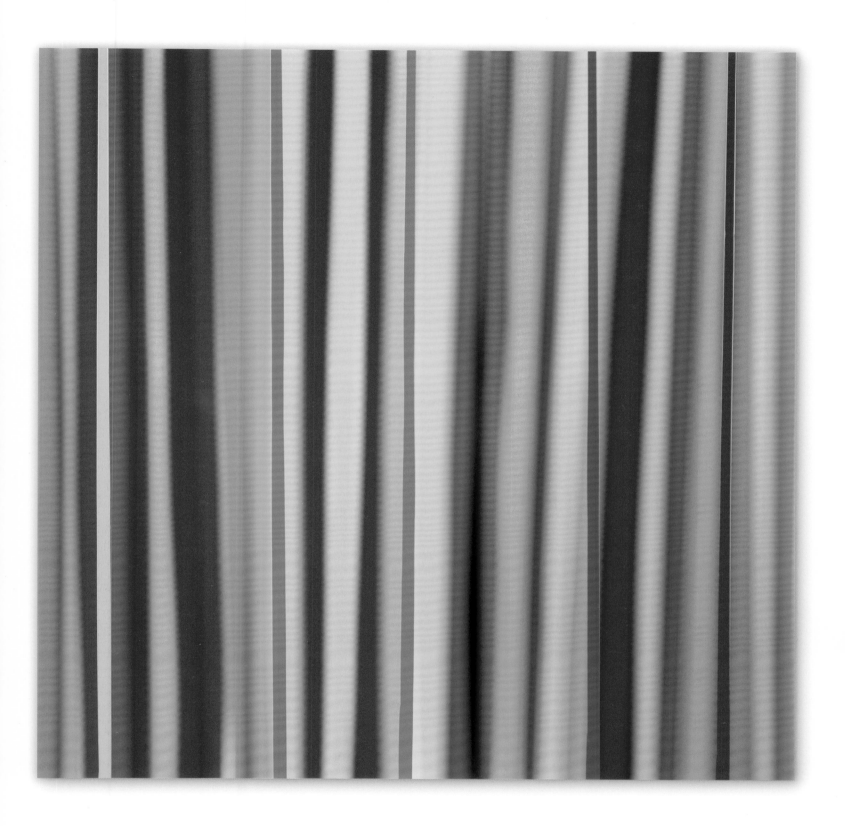

RN123 **Vertical Lines, Light and Paint**   2001
unique Cibachrome with paint mounted on aluminium and framed
29 × 29 in   74 × 74 cm

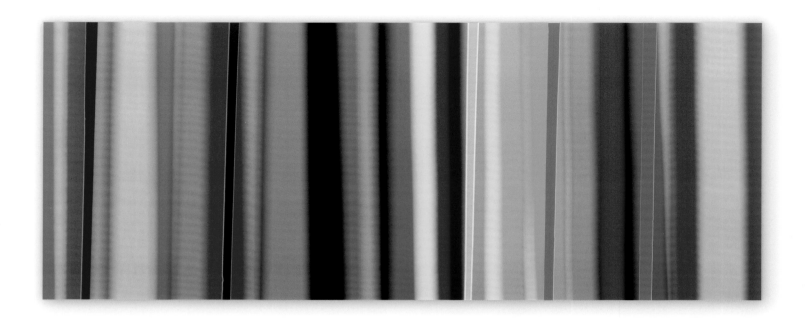

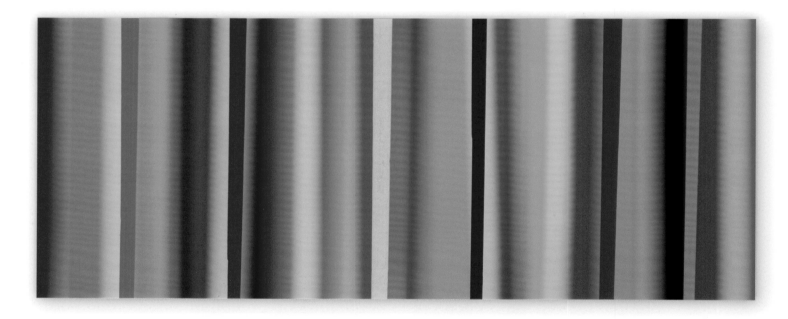

RN346 **Small Vertical Lines, Light and Paint**   2004
unique Cibachrome with paint mounted on aluminium and framed
24 × 12 in   61 × 30 cm

RN432 **Small Vertical Lines, Light and Paint**   2004
unique Cibachrome with paint mounted on aluminium and framed
24 × 12 in   61 × 30 cm

RN412 **Small Vertical Lines, Light and Paint**   2004
unique Cibachrome with paint mounted on aluminium and framed
24 × 12 in   61 × 30 cm

Coloured **Light Project**ions

RN753 **Coloured Light Projections**   2006
unique Cibachrome mounted on aluminium and framed
78 × 37 in   198 × 94 cm

RN639 **Coloured Light Projections**   2006
unique Cibachrome mounted on aluminium and framed
83 × 41 in   211 × 104 cm

RN609 **Coloured Light Projections** 2005
unique Cibachrome mounted on aluminium and framed
89 × 38 in 226 × 97 cm

RN529 **Coloured Light Projections** 2005
unique Cibachrome mounted on aluminium and framed
73 × 24 in 185 × 61 cm

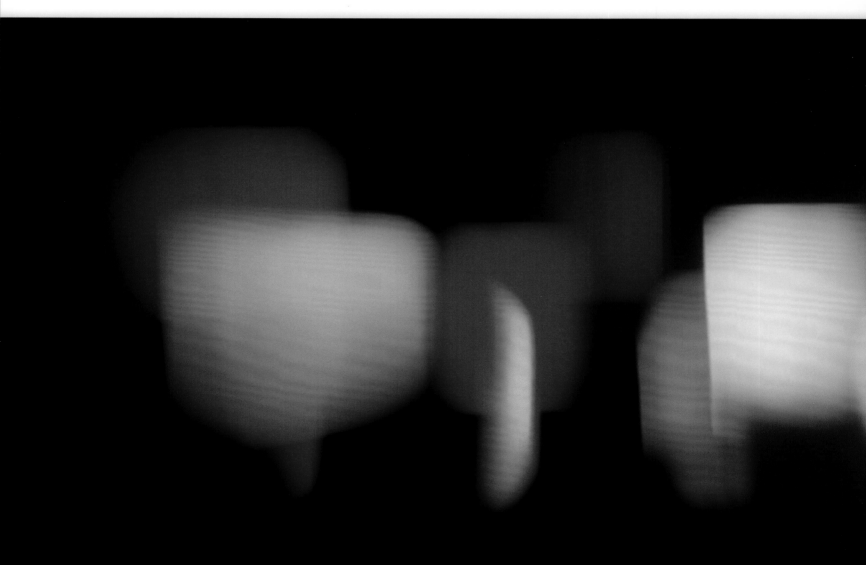

RN609 **Coloured Light Projections** 2005
unique Cibachrome mounted on aluminium and framed
89 × 38 in 226 × 97 cm

RN529 **Coloured Light Projections** 2005
unique Cibachrome mounted on aluminium and framed
73 × 24 in 185 × 61 cm

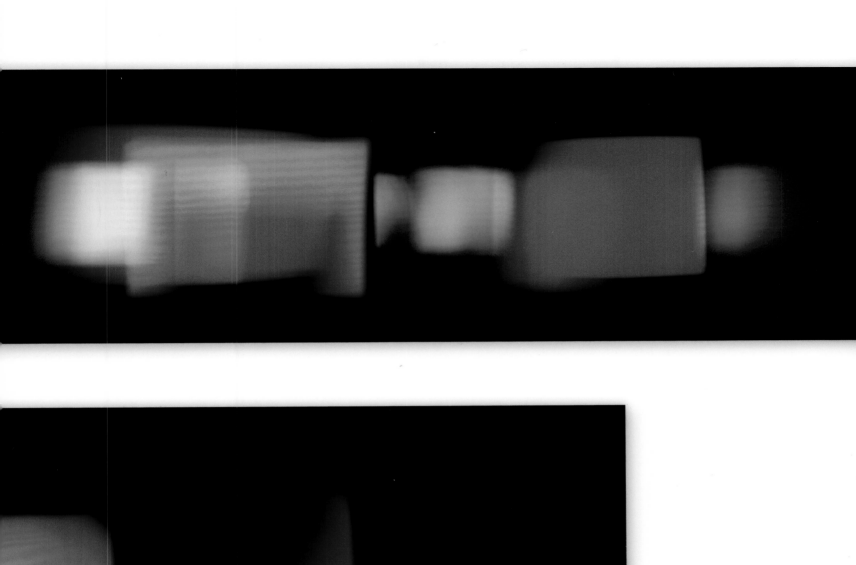

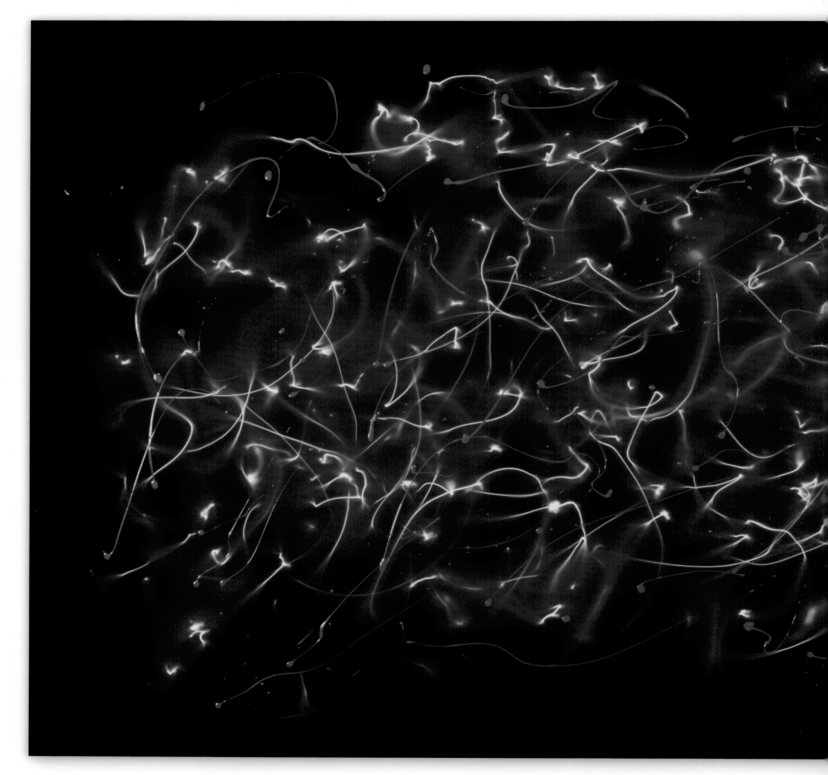

Light **Paint**ings

transformation has been a subtle but guiding force in many of their artworks, not only **Paint Pigment Photographs** but also in the act of appropriation in **Postcards From Vegas**, the revolving neon circles and the colour changing lights used in their exhibition at the Museum of Neon Art in Los Angeles. Even the Carters' early series, **Painting Photographs**, was dependent on the concept of transformation – from making something figurative become abstract and in the manipulation of boundaries between what is created by the artists and what is seen by the viewer. In their hands imagery is often in a state of transformation, from one medium to another and this heightens our visual appetite, presenting more than one way of looking and understanding.

The critical point of genesis for the exhibition **Transforming** was created between 2009 and 2012. **Transforming Still Life Painting**[178] takes as its subject a Dutch Golden Age masterpiece by Ambrosius Bosschaert the Elder. Working with MPC, the Carters created an animated version of Bosschaert's **Vase With Flowers in a Window**. Every aspect has been brought to life and the seamless three-hour loop takes the painted scene from dusk to dawn. Only perceptible upon sustained looking, the still life displays subtle shifts as the clouds pass by, the sun moves in the sky and the stars emerge. Each flower has been informed by actual time-lapse footage of real flowers throughout the course of the day, marking subtle shifts in bloom and direction as they turn to face the sun. Every few minutes the still life displays real-time activity, such as a caterpillar eating leaves. In their homage the artists examine the boundaries between the real and the imagined, analogue and digital, and the traditional and the progressive.

Their world first 'digital painting' provided a unique intersection between the worlds of Old Master connoisseurship and the dynamic world of contemporary new media art. It was selected by *The Art Newspaper* as a top five pick at TEFAF; an Old Master dealer who acquired an edition described it as "better than the real thing" in *The New York Times* and Sir Peter Blake, the eminent pop artist and avid collector, described it as the most important addition to his collection in the past decade. Despite its accolades (it is on permanent display at the Manchester Museum of Art; it will be on display at New York's

Frick Collection from October 2013 to January 2014 and has been accepted into the Mauritshuis permanent collection) it has not yet been part of a Rob and Nick Carter exhibition and will be an important anchor for the show.

Joining it will be three new time-based media works made with MPC that adopt an Old Master painting in a groundbreaking form of homage. **Transforming Vanitas Painting**[190] (2013) is based on the 1630 oil on copper **Dead Frog with Flies** by Ambrosius Bosschaert the Younger. In the three-hour sequence the Carters underscore the sensitive presentation of *vanitas* by taking the scene from the last few minutes of the creature's life through various stages of decay and ultimate decomposition. The genius of the Carters' vision is that it captures the decaying frog, but the viewer is always conscious that visually this is very much a painted frog. Every brushstroke and texture is captured and the entire scene treated not as a biological survey into decomposition, but as a moving, 'living' painting. This is *vanitas* painting for the twenty-first century.

Transforming Diptych[202] (2013) brings to life a pair of still life paintings by Justus Juncker dating from 1765. The Carters have drawn inspiration from the monumental and mysterious presentation of the fruits by Juncker. Their work ostensibly appears to be two independently framed, quiet paintings. Sustained looking reveals that not only have the Carters brought the scenes alive, they have created a deep interconnection. As a butterfly leaves one frame, it disappears into the space of gallery wall and reappears moments later on the other fruit. In line with their previous interest in chance and unpredictability, the Carters have directed MPC to develop sophisticated programming that results in a cycle of activity unlikely to be predicted or seen in exactly the same order.

The artists have also taken on the challenge of Giorgione's **Sleeping Venus** in **Transforming Nude Painting**[212] (2013). The Carters have breathed life into the masterpiece, transporting the viewer to the Venetian landscape where Venus peacefully sleeps as the day passes. In a similar vein to the gentle passage of time in **Transforming Still Life Painting**, the scene passes from dawn to dusk imperceptibly. This is a deeply evocative, highly naturalistic presentation

This was succinctly embodied with another neon series, **Read Colours Not Words**[96] (2009) that was installed on Islington High Street. It is formed of six rows of seven words. Each was made of neon and spelled a different colour such as RED or BLUE, but each was created with a colour of neon at odds with the word. For instance the letters that spell ORANGE might glow in bright blue neon. Here, as with all of their work, the Carters put colour (not words) first. **Public Perception of Colour**[128] (2009) continued with the theme of how we read colour and marked their first foray into public participation. The viewer was invited to select a Pantone colour sample that they felt best represented a word such as 'red'. The diverse results could not be predicted and serve as a compelling exploration into how radically different our understanding of colour can be.

It has long been written that Rob and Nick Carter's work is centered on the possibilities of colour, light and form. This was certainly true and integral to their earliest series and remains important. However, what has emerged is a larger, over-reaching concern that has propelled their artwork forward into new and even more engaging territory. That is the notion of perception and how we engage with and see a work of art. They underscore this by examining how they might deliver visual transformations in their practice to better emphasise the viewer's position in the dynamic between the artwork and its reception.

Several of their neon works came to be fashioned as large-scale permanent installations such as **Revolution in Two Parts**[86] (2010) at Aldersgate opposite the Museum of London, **Wavelength**[84] (2006) in Victoria and **Wavelength Through Blue**[92] (2009) in Savile Row. The works in neon are not just a development in medium, they also marked an interesting departure into movement. Each utilises the possibility of programming the work to change, either revolving through colour spectrums or activating moving neon light by nearby movement, thus presenting the viewer with a constantly evolving visual experience.

each combination coheres in a subtle fashion and avoids disjuncture with careful mirroring and visual echoes. The results are surprising: far from jarring the neon series speak of the pre-digital era whilst simultaneously presenting a highly original and contemporary aesthetic.

The Carters have always allowed room for a level of unpredictability in their practice – the failure rate of many of the light paintings was incredibly high, especially for the intricate **Spectrum Circles** series made using fine light sources and a spinning potter's wheel. Chance became a more seriously incorporated component in two series made outside of the studio and both involving paint in 2012, **Unconscious Paintings**[114] and **Paint Pigment Photographs**[132]. **Unconscious Paintings** are entirely dependent on chance as the majority of the creative act happens completely outside of the artists' hands. The experimental series is a development of the surrealist notion of unconscious painting. Small bottles of paint lean precariously over the edges of a clean canvas prepared by the Carters. The paint does not unleash its potential until after the piece is sent via Royal Mail, encased in a Perspex box and hidden in a shipping crate. Each work is formed of one colour and is sent with instructions to an international museum with the objective being that it is returned to sender. Exposed to random, incalculable activity, the concept subverts the traditional relationship between artist and artwork, the artwork and museum and the limits between paint, canvas and sculpture.

Paint Pigment Photographs neatly demonstrate the artists' preoccupation with light, colour and form and the series is underscored by chance and unpredictability. The Hindu festival of Holi inspired the action photography that captures paint pigment spontaneously thrown into the air. Explosions of coloured pigment captured at 1/8000th of a second retain the energy of the act itself, suspended in space. The resulting photograph, no easy thing to create, is a physical manifestation of the actual performance, creating an imprint of the spontaneous and unrepeatable gesture. The series plays on the transient nature of light and form, and also creates a dialogue about the ephemeral aspect of art. The genesis of the series is in the transformative act of throwing the pigment – turning a static painting ingredient into an active gesture and recording a split second of its time suspended against the clouds.

The 2013 exhibition for which this book has been compiled, presents a new body of work that has been over three years in the making with the notion of transforming at its core. However, the theme of

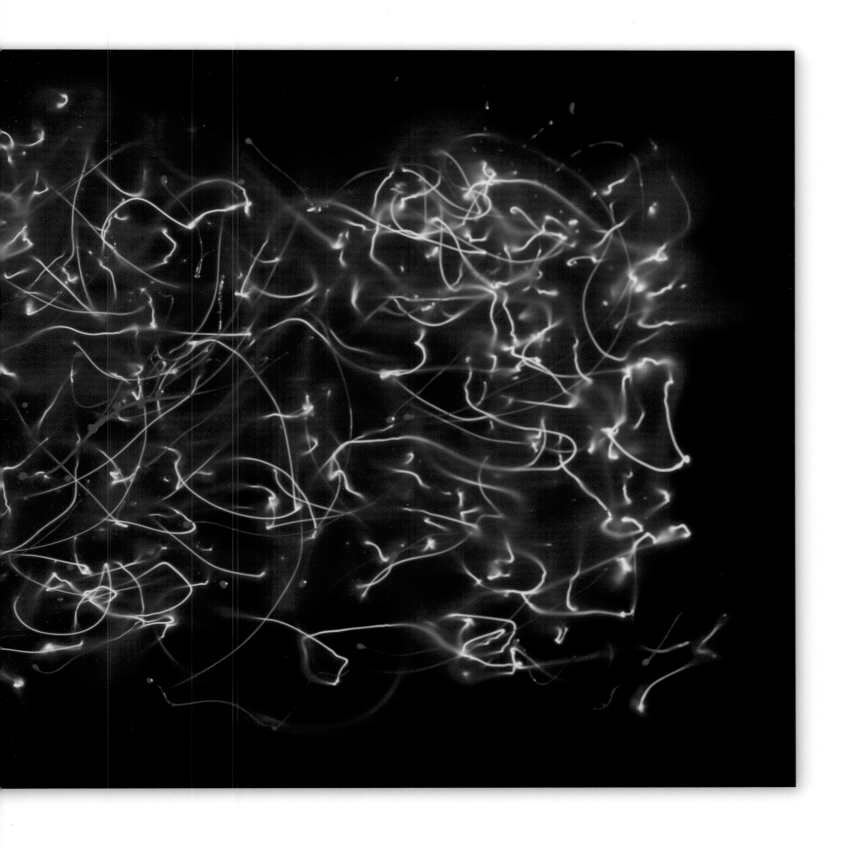

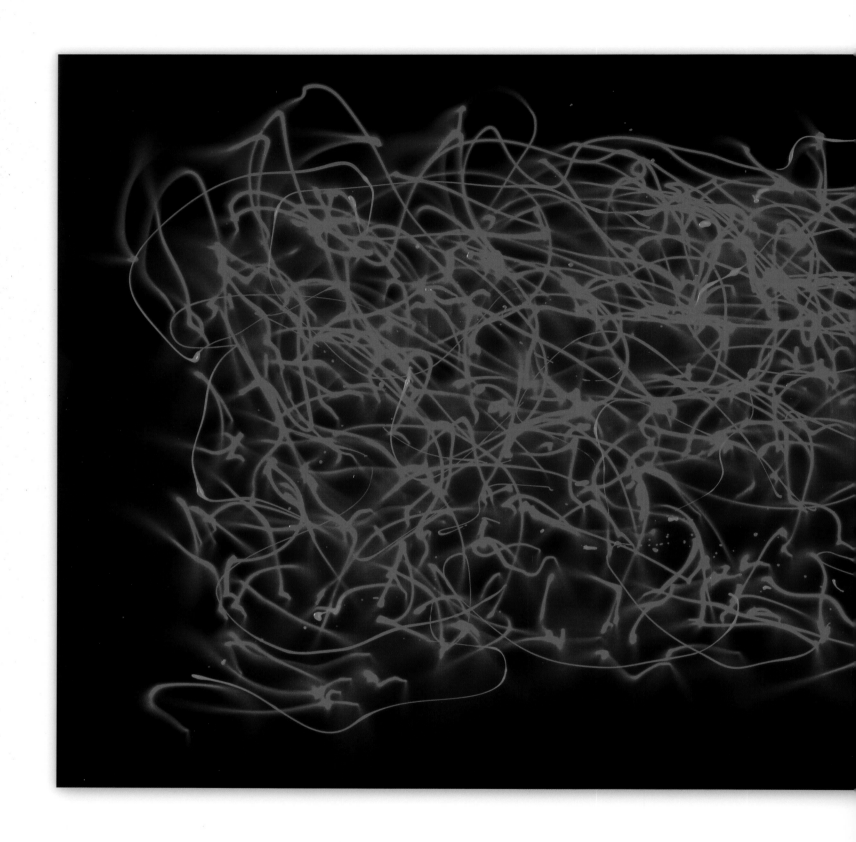

RN243 **Light Painting Dragon's Blood Red**   2003
unique Cibachrome with paint mounted on aluminium and framed
91 × 46 in   231 × 117 cm

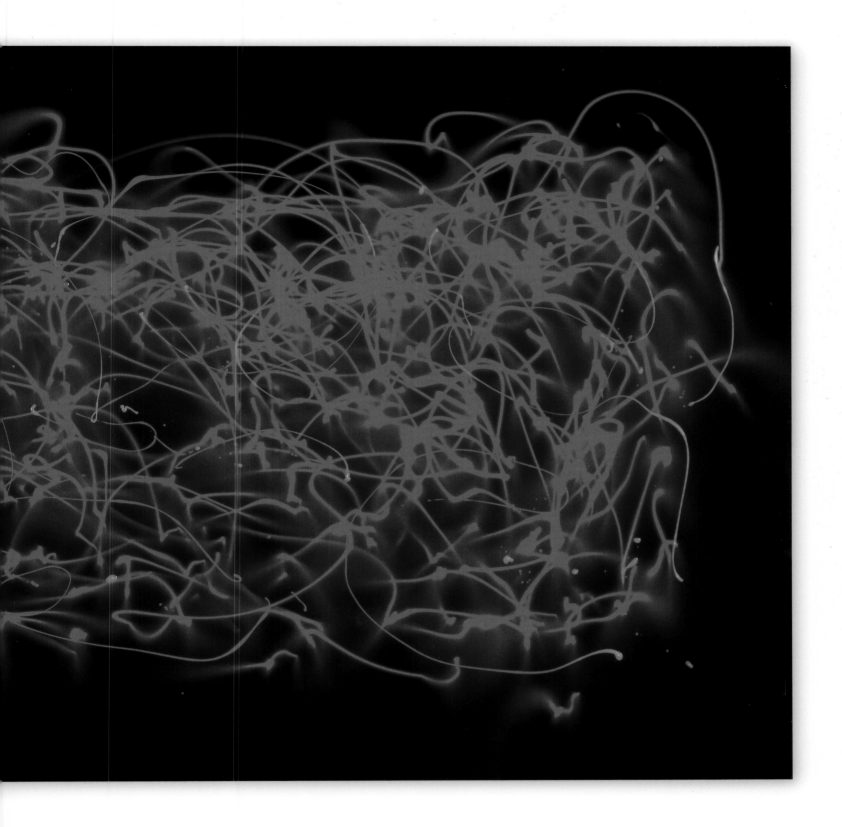

FOLLOWING PAGES

RN22 **Light Painting Blue**   1999   DETAIL
unique Cibachrome with paint mounted on aluminium and framed
84 × 32 in   213 × 81 cm

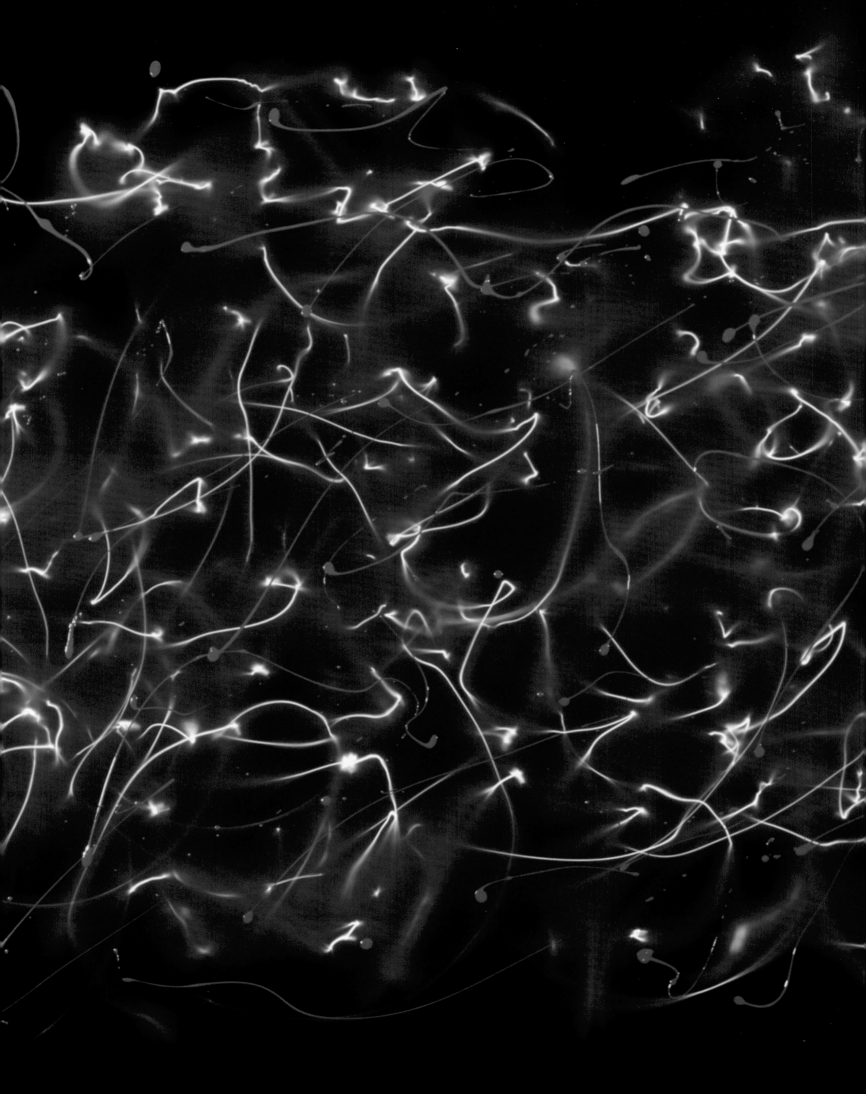

Approached with a different aesthetic perspective these could just as easily be gestural paintings – they're certainly very experimental and the Carters have an almost Greenbergian love of the intrinsic qualities of the light, just as an artist may have the joy of the paint.

The basis of the process is in fact, technically speaking, photographic, in that it's an image produced by means of chemical action of light from fibre optics onto sensitive film. But photography has nothing to do with it. These colour-kinetic lights are used like great squeegees across the surface of the sensitised ground, a process that describes itself in the newer works almost in a Richteresque manner. Interestingly these same lights used in the process are also projected back onto the finished piece in order to create the works' changing colours as they scroll through the spectrum.

Up until my studio visit I'd only seen the work in catalogues, and in reproduction it loses well over fifty percent – not necessarily of vibrancy, though this suffers too – but more of its status as something that moves in harmony with specific light changes to create the overall effect.

At first the work seems to have obvious visual associations with Pop and Op art – certain pieces more than others. The early target paintings for instance would seem to follow a Pop tradition, but are probably more informed by the visual heritage of pop art itself than any ongoing examination of the mass culture that characterised the movement of Pop. It's closer perhaps to Op art, but while these works may draw you into

wondering how the artists have achieved certain visual effects, neither Rob or Nick Carter – who operate with an equal strength of vision – have set out to trick the eye. The work in fact is totally unambiguous. It is purely formal, referring to itself in its intentions.

Colour is the fundamental aspect, employing form to maximise its impact and vibrancy. What gives the work its freshness and something unexpected is perhaps its experimental nature. The entire process is conducted in complete darkness where the image is gradually built up by added increments of light. Working in darkness, the element of surprise is in a sense expected. There are no indications as to what they will have until later, when the work is processed. Some of the effects achieved by default have now been adopted much in the same way as Bacon became specific about his accidental processes, refined and honed over the years.

One of the lasting effects you take away with you is similar in kind to having been blinded by high-wattage lamps. Afterwards, when you close your eyes, candescent lights float about on your retina, creating not so much an exact facsimile of the work but an impression of its power.

Harland Miller   Artist

Multi-coloured Lines

RN334 **Pink Lines**   2004
unique Cibachrome mounted on aluminium
30 × 60 in   76 × 152 cm

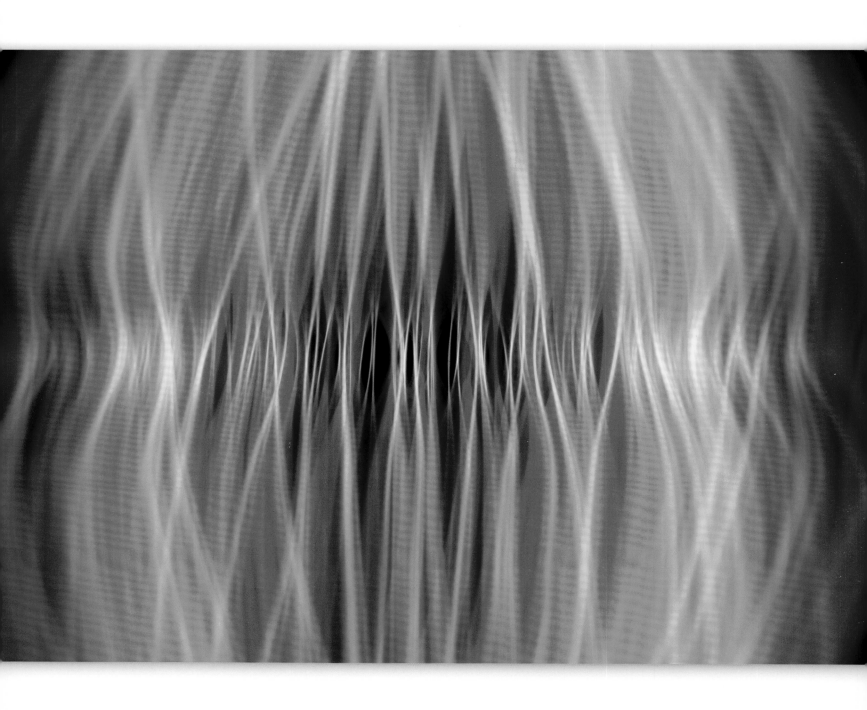

RN428 **Multi-coloured Lines**   2004
unique Cibachrome mounted on aluminium and framed
71 × 50 in   180 × 127 cm

RN429 **Blue Lines** 2004
unique Cibachrome mounted on aluminium and framed
77 × 51 in   196 × 130 cm

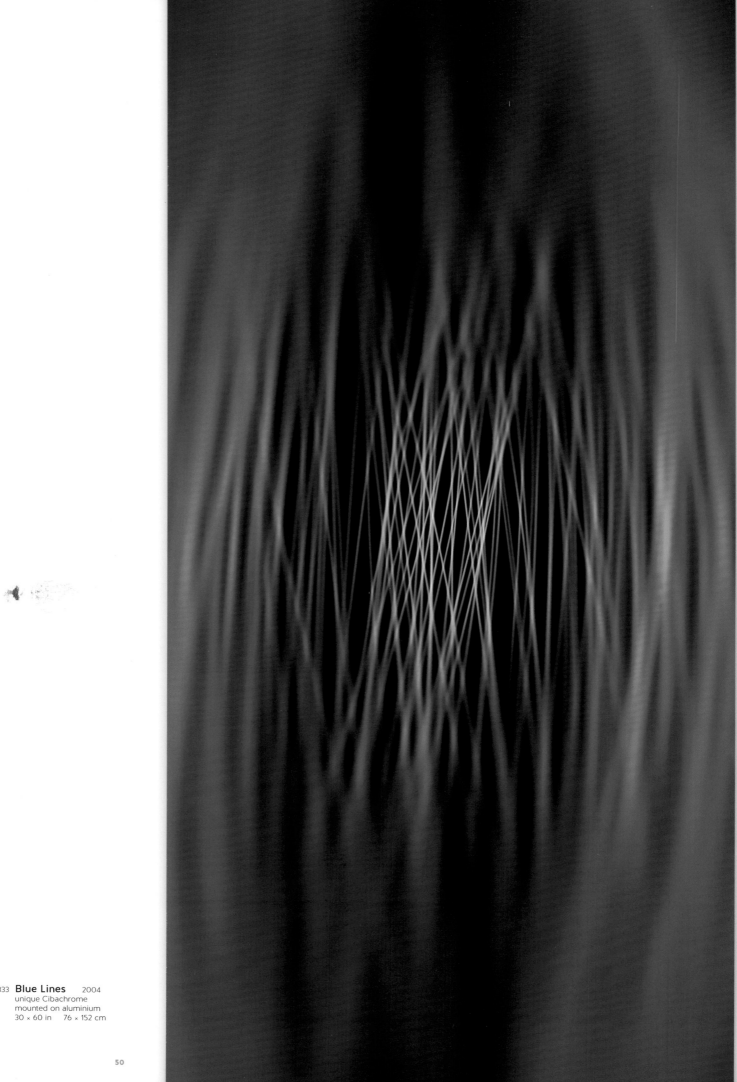

RN333 **Blue Lines** 2004
unique Cibachrome
mounted on aluminium
30 × 60 in   76 × 152 cm

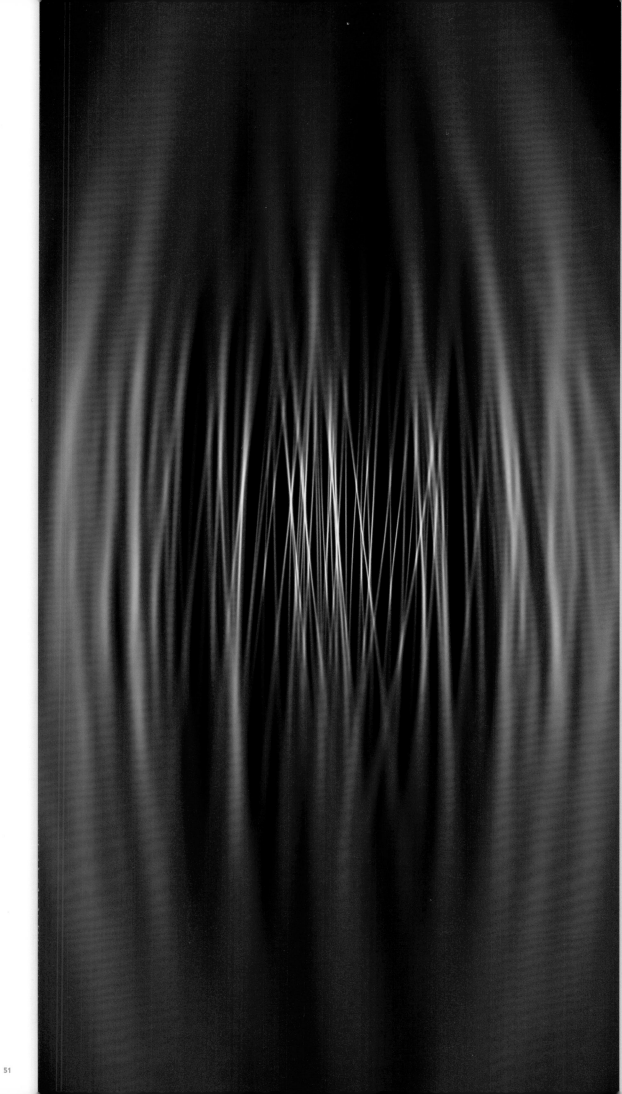

RN335 **Purple Lines** 2004
unique Cibachrome
mounted on aluminium
30 × 60 in 76 × 152 cm

Colour Spirals

RN771 **Colour Changing Spiral** 2010
unique Cibachrome mounted on aluminium and framed
36 × 44 in   91 × 112 cm

RN398 **Colour Changing Spiral** 2004
unique Cibachrome mounted on aluminium and framed
30 × 37 in   76 × 94 cm

RN382 **Colour Changing Spiral** 2004
unique Cibachrome mounted on aluminium and framed
34 × 41 in   86 × 104 cm

RN383 **Colour Changing Spiral** 2004
unique Cibachrome mounted on aluminium and framed
32 × 36 in   81 × 91 cm

RN308 **Colour Changing Spiral** 2003
unique Cibachrome mounted on aluminium and framed
50 × 60 in   127 × 152 cm

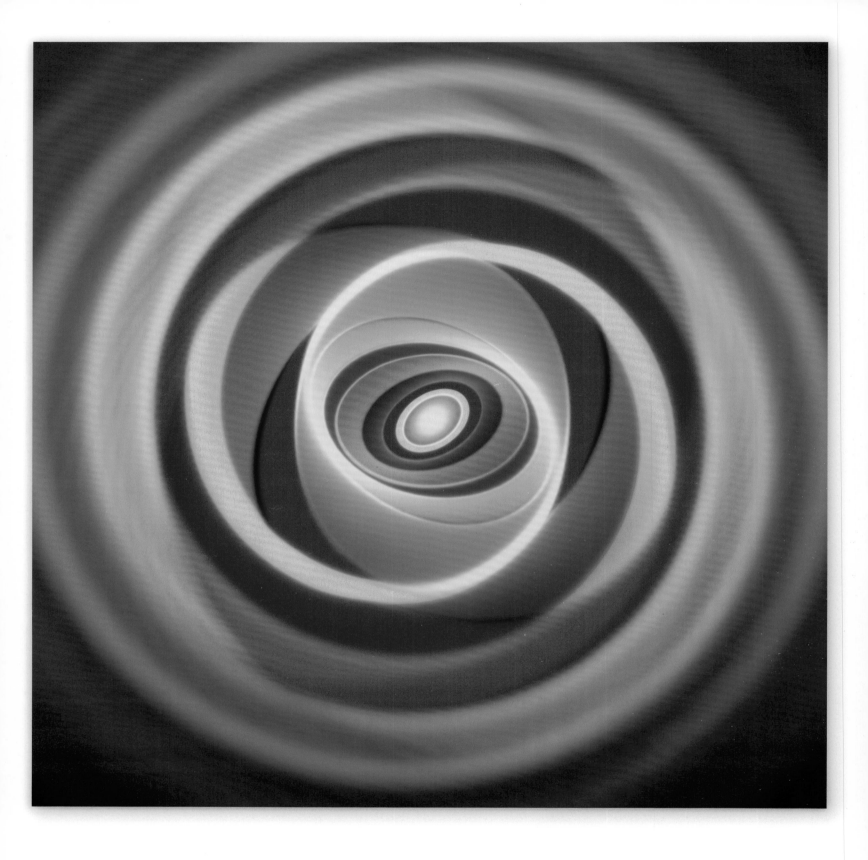

RN374 **Colour Spiral** 2004
unique Cibachrome mounted on aluminium and framed
45 × 45 in   114 × 114 cm

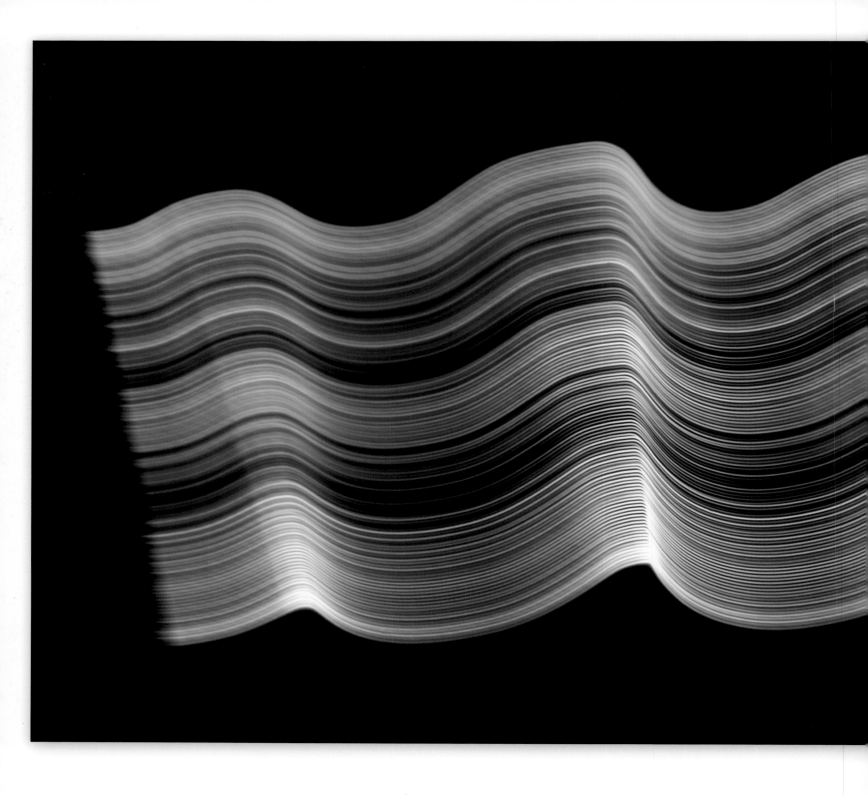

RN174 **Light Drawing Peppermint** 2002
unique Cibachrome mounted on aluminium and framed
44 × 19 in   112 × 48 cm

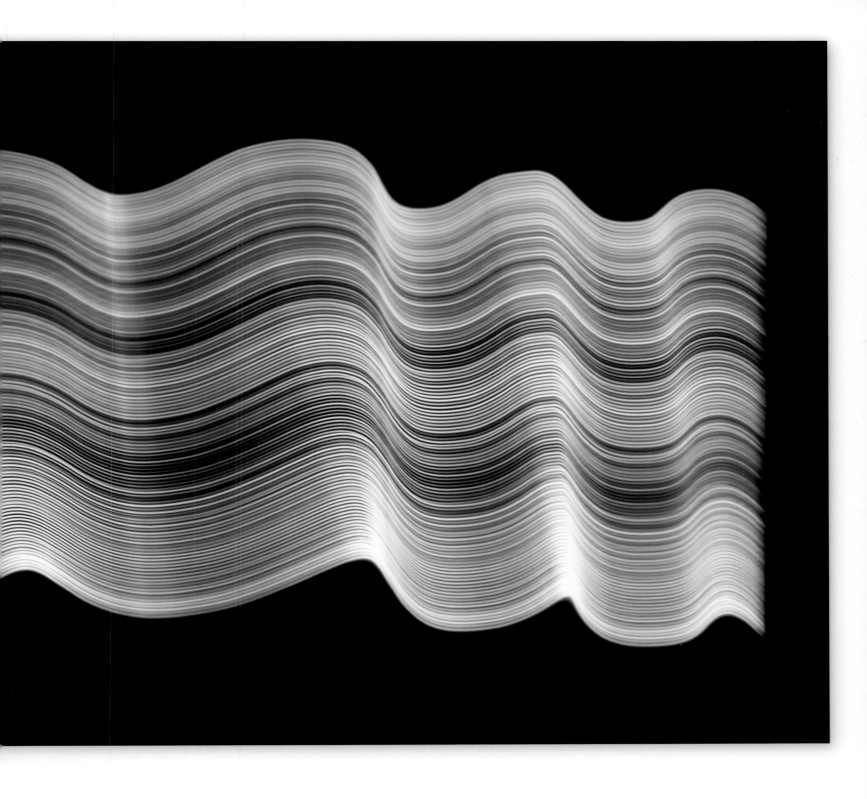

Light Drawings

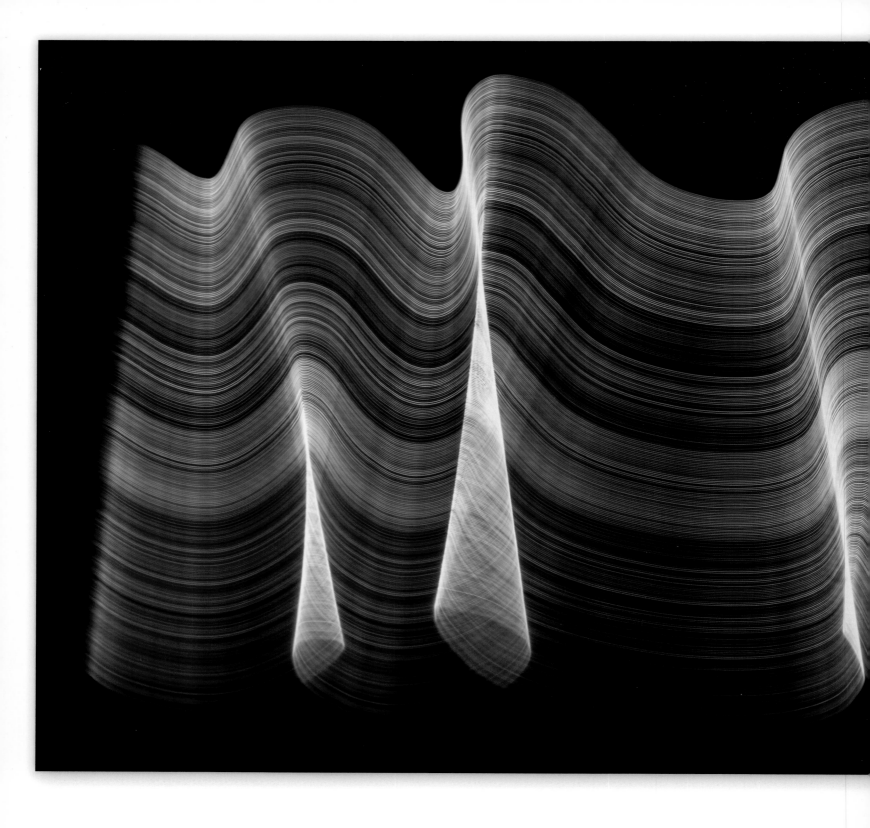

RN151 **Light Drawing Mauve**   2002
unique Cibachrome mounted on aluminium and framed
94 × 37 in   239 × 94 cm

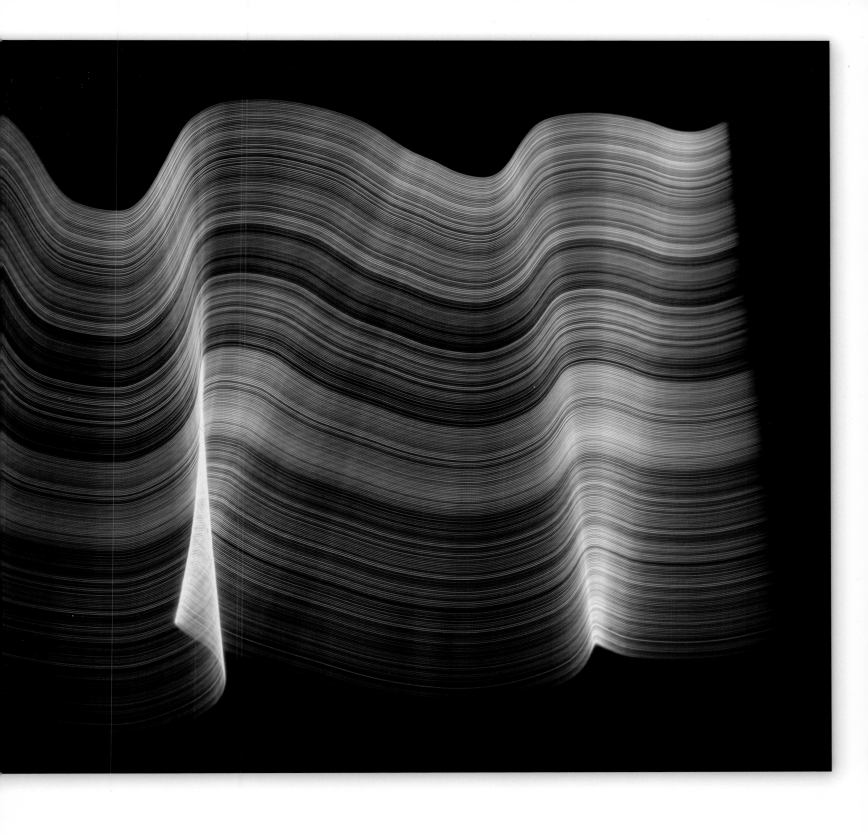

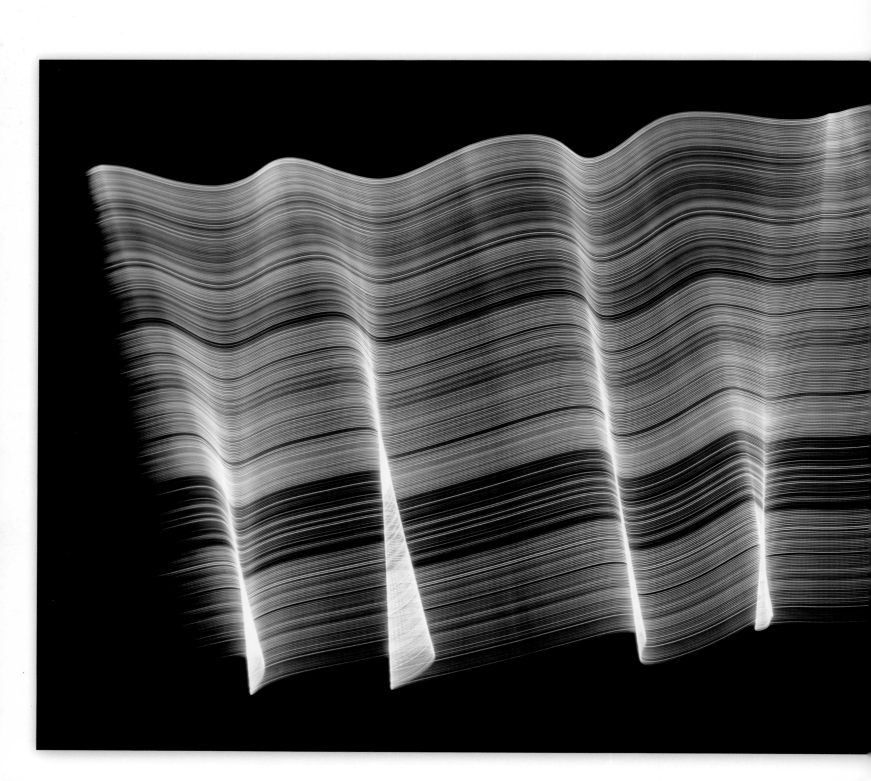

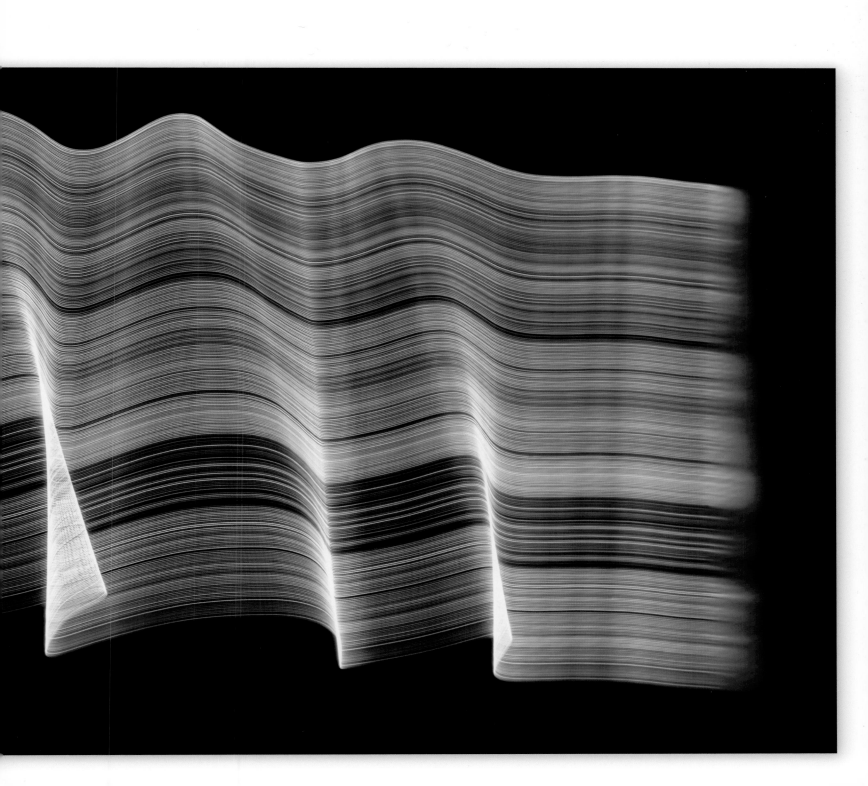

RN268 **Neon, Clear Red, Blue Glass Coated Turquoise Pumped Blue** 2003
unique Cibachrome mounted on aluminium
48 × 22 in   122 × 56 cm

Neon Landscapes

RN658 **Neon, Green Glass, Clear Blue**   2007
unique Cibachrome mounted on aluminium
95 × 21½ in   241 × 55 cm

RN661 **Neon, Clear Blue, Bright Blue** 2007
unique Cibachrome mounted on aluminium
89 × 47 in   226 × 119 cm

Mag Lights

RN381 **Mag Light, Multi-Coloured** 2004
unique Cibachrome mounted on aluminium and framed
45 × 39 in   114 × 99 cm

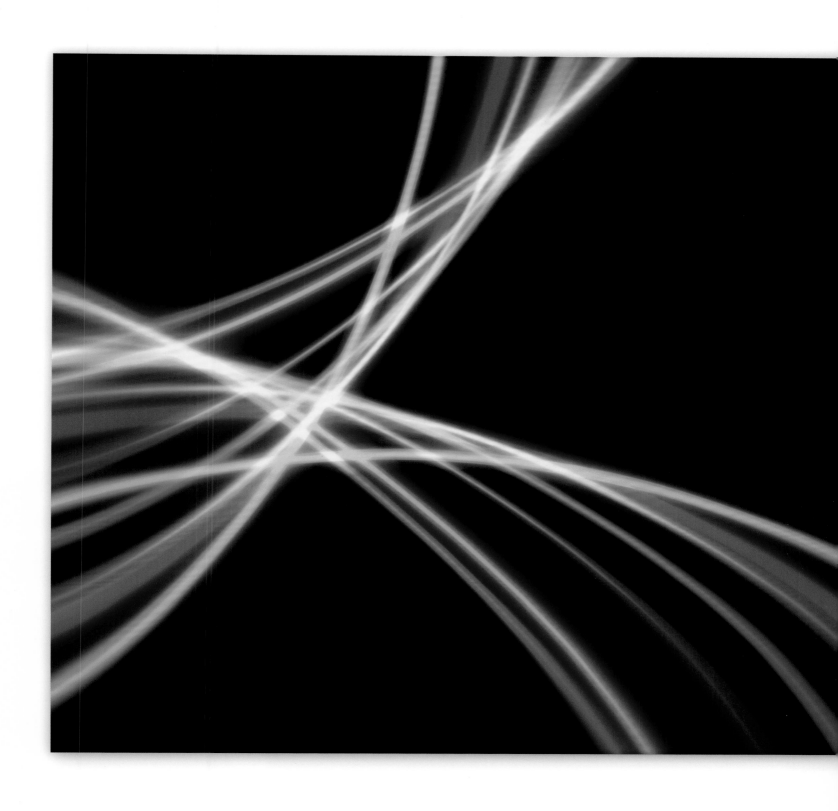

RN420 **Mag Light, Multi-Coloured** 2004
unique Cibachrome mounted on aluminium and framed
52 × 46 in   132 × 117 cm

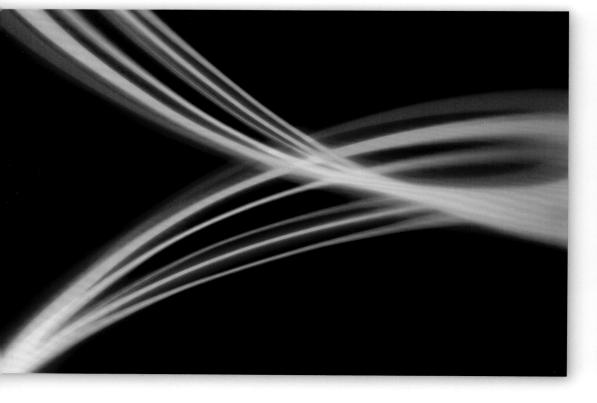

RN430 **Mag Light, Multi-Coloured, Triptych** 2004
3 unique Cibachrome prints mounted on aluminium
each 79 × 47 in 201 × 119 cm

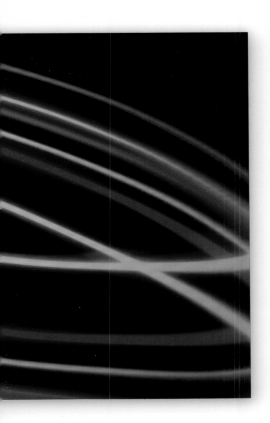
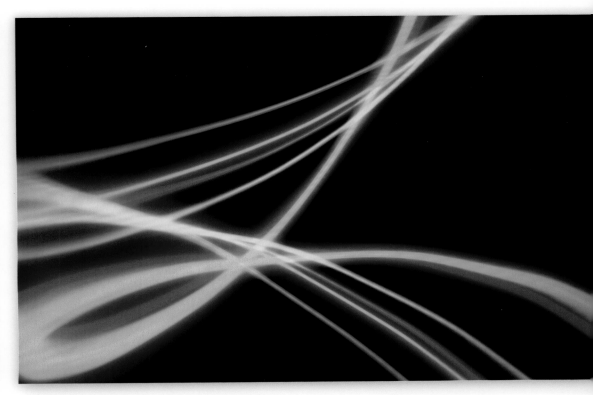

RN425 **Mag Light, Multi-Coloured** 2004
unique Cibachrome mounted on aluminium and framed
71 × 50 in   180 × 127 cm

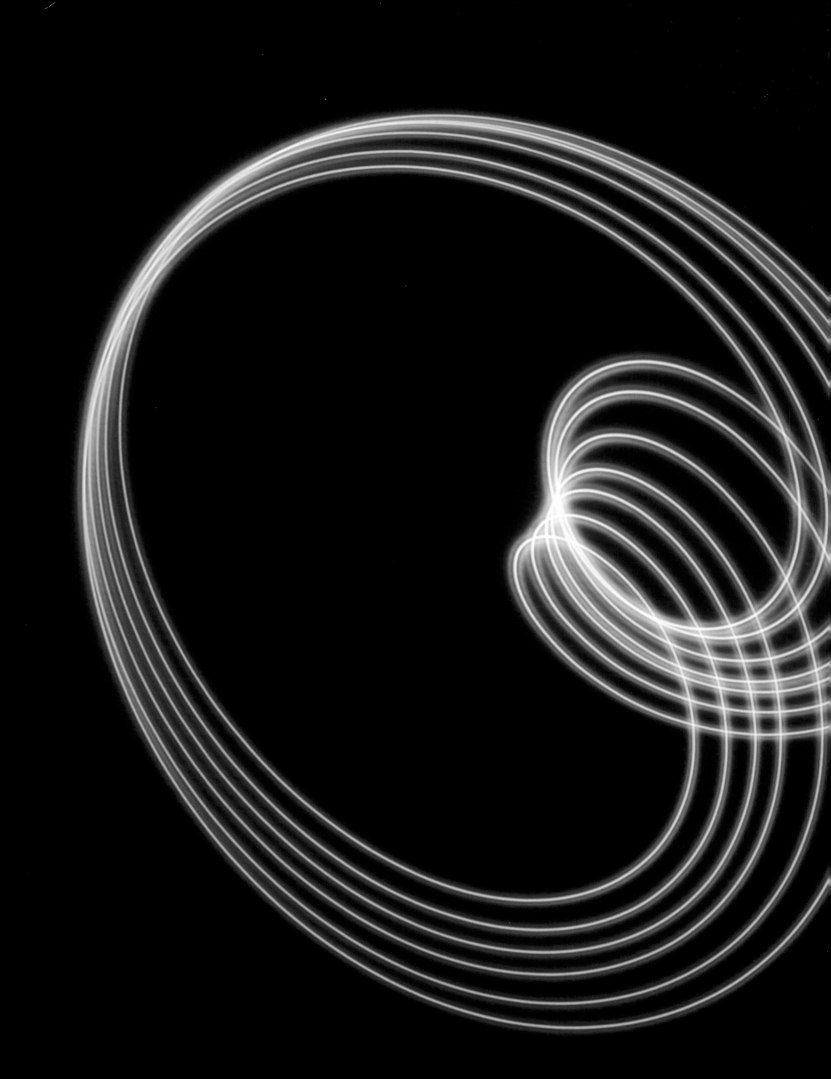

This work is a unique drawing with light. It is part of
a series using patterns created by the harmonograph,
a Victorian scientific device used to trace mathematic
intervals that occur in music and other wave forms.
Rob and Nick Carter made their own contemporary
version of a harmonograph to create this pattern,
which is called a 'rotary octave'. The result speaks of
invisible forces and universal physical laws.

Martin Barnes   Senior Curator   Photographs
Victoria and Albert Museum

Harmonographs

RN622 **Continuous Line Drawing, Harmonograph, VI**   2006
unique Cibachrome mounted on aluminium and framed
36 × 36 in   91 × 91 cm

RN617 **Continuous Line Drawing, Harmonograph, I** 2006
unique Cibachrome print mounted on aluminium and framed
36 × 36 in   91 × 91 cm

RN621 **Continuous Line Drawing, Harmonograph, V**   2006
unique Cibachrome mounted on aluminium and framed
36 × 36 in   91 × 91 cm

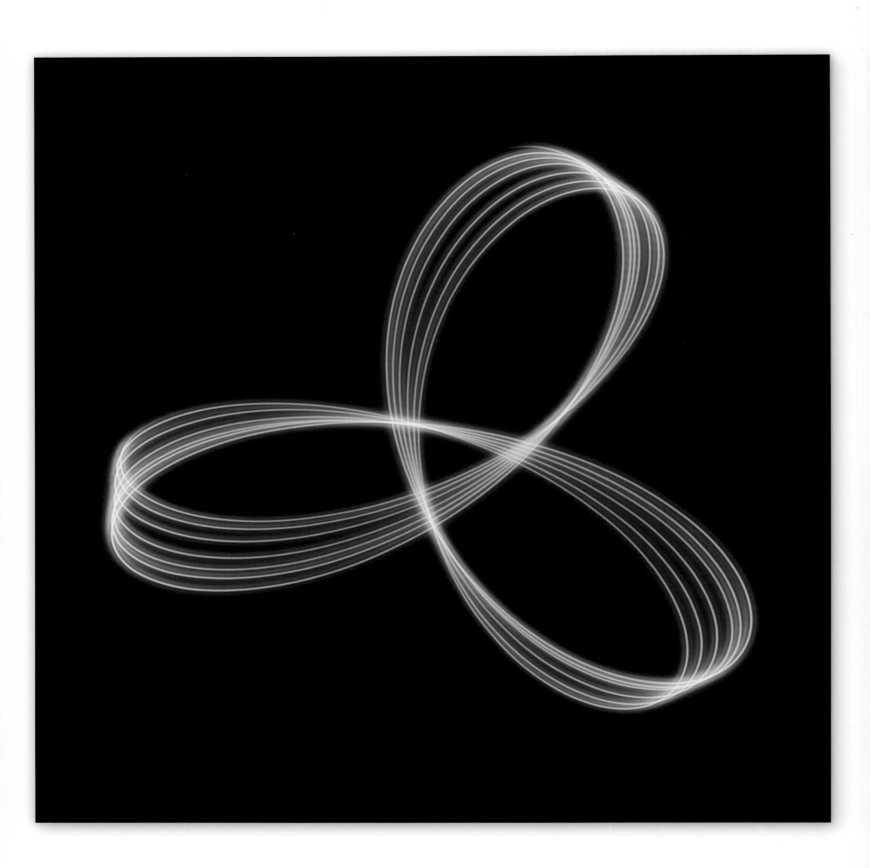

RN618 **Continuous Line Drawing, Harmonograph, II**   2006
unique Cibachrome mounted on aluminium and framed
36 × 36 in   91 × 91 cm

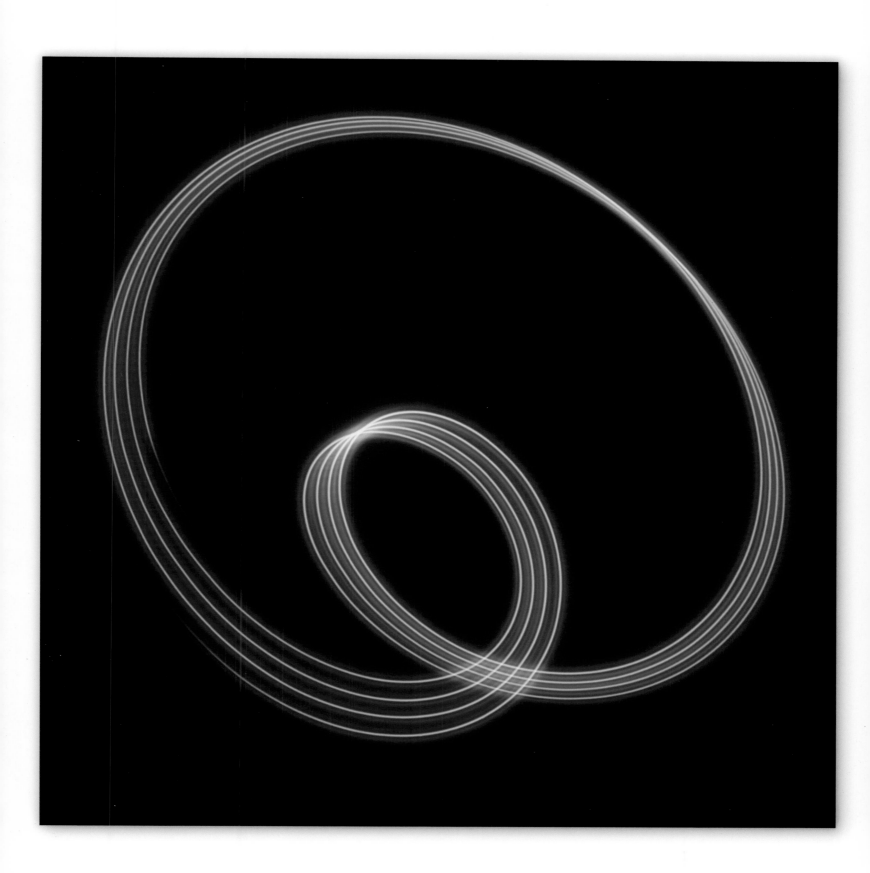

RN620 **Continuous Line Drawing, Harmonograph, IV** 2006
unique Cibachrome mounted on aluminium and framed
36 × 36 in 91 × 91 cm

RN698 **Continuous Line Drawing, Harmonograph, III**   2006
unique Cibachrome print mounted on aluminium and framed
36 × 36 in   91 × 91 cm

The Carters' neon installations at the museum are a retinal feast of pulsating hues and a feast for the soul. My response to the installation was similar to the first time I experienced the Aurora Borealis, except I wasn't outdoors in Alaska, but in a small room in downtown L.A. How do you describe this work to someone? Yes, the colours both leapt forward off the picture plane and receded back into it. The colours had a centering effect, they were still but in motion. If one could capture nature's colour in a room it would look like these rhythmic and almost magical pulsating rings of pure colour.

Kim Koga
Director   Museum of Neon Art   California

Neon Light Works

RN924 **Wavelength**   2006
152 movement-activated neon tubes
71 × 106 in   180 × 270 cm

RN792 **Revolution in Two Parts** 2010
unique double-sided colour changing neon lightboxes
each 98 in ø   250 cm ø

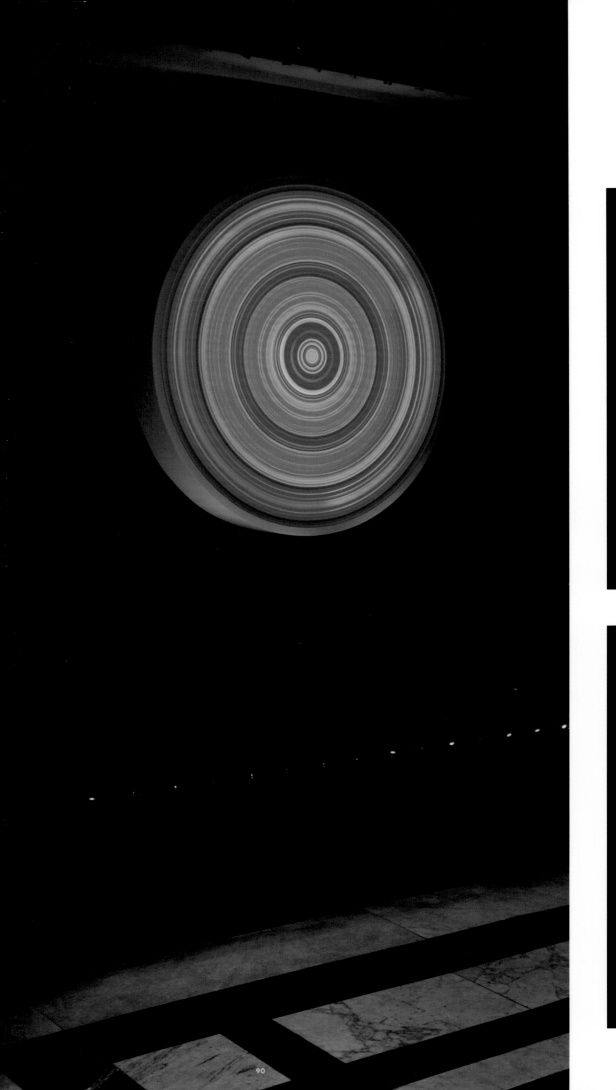
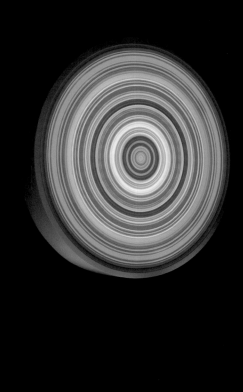

RN754 **Colour Changing Lightbox**   2010
unique Cibachrome transparency backlit with 15 concentric circles of neon
colour changing sequence
fully programmable
52 ø × 6 in   132 ø × 5 cm

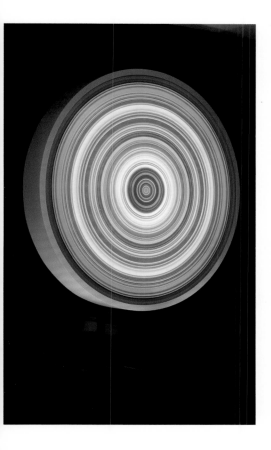

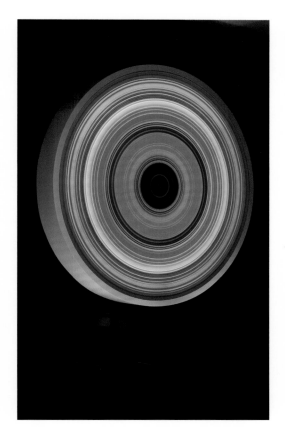

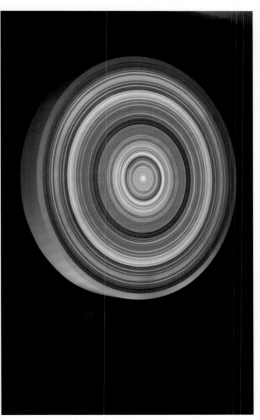

RN926 **Wavelength Through Blue**   2009
150 movement-activated neon tubes
590 × 39 in   1500 × 100 cm

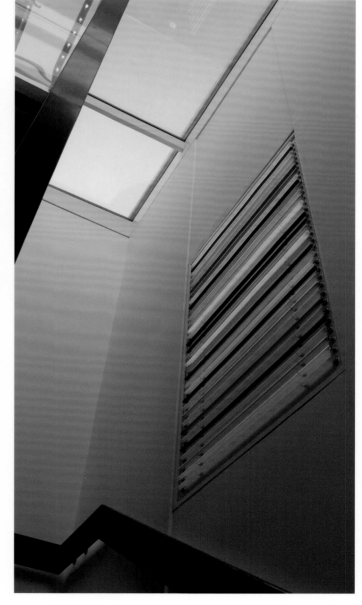

RN925 **Wavelength in Three Parts** 2008
3 panels of movement-activated neons
each panel 44½ × 46½ in   113 × 118 cm

RN928 **Read Colours Not Words, From Blue to Orange**   2009   DETAIL
unique multi-coloured neon
118 × 47 × 8 in   300 × 120 × 20 cm

Read Colours Not Words, From Green to Yellow   2009
unique multi-coloured neon
240 × 138 × 8 in   610 × 350 × 20 cm

I loved **Read Colours Not Words** the moment I saw it. As well as collecting modern art, I've always had an interest in magic, illusion and psychological games and here was something that combined both worlds in a way that was both witty and rather beautiful.

The work is based on the delightfully named 'Stroop Effect' which demonstrates that the brain finds it difficult to cope with two conflicting tasks – that is, to read out the word BLUE when that word is actually red or green. I'm not quite sure what the point of the experiment is, but I remember finding examples of the Stroop Effect in books of illusions that I was given as a child and they always amused me then.

I also love the medium that Rob and Nick have chosen – neon lighting – as it takes me back to another age. I'm sure that the giant billboards in New York's Times Square and London's Piccadilly Circus were all neon-lit back in the twenties and there are still some wonderful examples of ads that edge towards art in places like Reno and Las Vegas (here once again, for me, the association is with magic – it's hard to think of Siegfried and Roy without pink neon). I feel that I grew up with neon but nowadays, all too often, I walk down streets, surrounded by coloured plastic fascias with

electric bulbs behind. There is very little magic to be found in the entrance to a McDonalds or a late night corner shop. Why did neon die out?

Even though the colours of neon lighting (in fact achieved by the use of different gases) are brilliant, they have an extraordinary softness. Nothing else glows quite like them. I've always been a fan of the American artist Dan Flavin because visiting an exhibition of his work manages to be both extraordinarily calming and inspiring. Other artists – Tracey Emin for one – have used neon to shock, twisting the noble gas into the much less noble sentiments of Mills & Boon romance with occasional expletives attached. Well, good for them – but I have always preferred art that makes me smile – and that's where Rob and Nick begin.

I wonder if **Read Colours Not Words** is a temporary installation? Surely, one day, the glass will crack, the gas will leak and all that will be left is an empty frame. This is something that Flavin himself seemed to accept. "Permanence defies everything," he once said. But I can live with that. In the end, after all, for all of us, the lights will have to go out.

Anthony Horowitz   Author

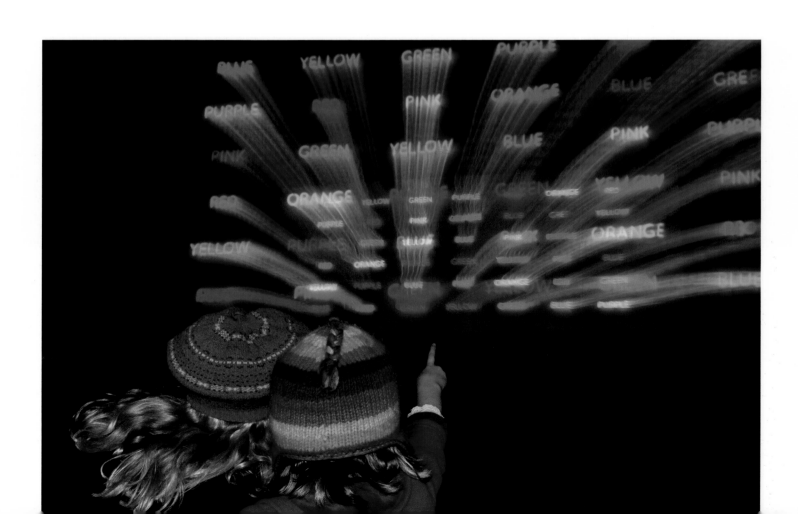

Read Colours Not Words, From Green to Yellow   2009
unique multi-coloured neon
240 × 138 × 8 in   610 × 350 × 20 cm

RN929 **Read Colours Not Words, From Blue to Yellow**   2009
unique multi-coloured neon
69 × 35½ × 4 in   175 × 90 × 10 cm

Rob and Nick are infuriatingly creative and we are
firm believers in their continually evolving practice.
Just when you think they have reached the pinnacle of
their creativity, they produce something entirely new.

We clearly recall our visit to The Fine Art Society
when we first encountered the Orb that we had heard
so much about. **Through Blue** is truly mesmerising,
hypnotic almost. We bought the artwork in a heartbeat
and have had many tranquil evenings wrapped in
its glow.

Martin and **Lesley Reith**   Collectors

Orbs

RN760 **Through Blue, Colour Changing Lightbox**   2010
unique lightbox
3 concentric circles of neon in 3 shades programmed to slowly fade between different blues
43 ø × 8½ in   109 ø × 22 cm

Painting Photographs

RN466 **Painting Photograph, Oil** 2004/5
framed Cibachrome print
49 × 59 in   124 × 150 cm
edition of 6

RN463 **Painting Photograph, Oil** 2004/5
framed Cibachrome print
49 × 59 in   124 × 150 cm
edition of 6

RN456 **Painting Photograph, Oil**   2004/5
framed Cibachrome print
49 × 59 in   124 × 150 cm
edition of 6

Unconscious Paintings

RN894 **Unconscious Painting, TATE**   2012
oil on canvas in perspex case
27 × 33 × 7 in   69 × 83 × 18 cm
posted Friday 29 June 2012
arrived Monday 9 July 2012

RN895 **Unconscious Painting, LACMA** 2012
oil on canvas in perspex case
27 × 33 × 7 in   69 × 83 × 18 cm
posted Friday 29 June 2012
arrived Monday 17 July 2012

RN898 **Unconscious Painting, Museum of Western Art, Tokyo** 2012
oil on canvas in perspex case
27 × 33 × 7 in   69 × 83 × 18 cm
posted Friday 29 June 2012
arrived Wednesday 24 September 2012

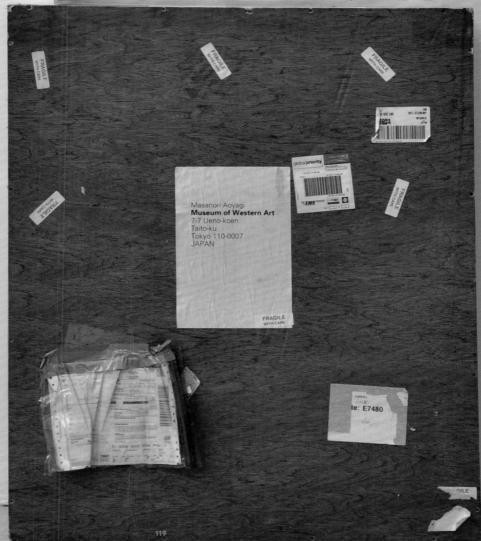

Masanori Aoyagi
Museum of Western Art
7-7 Ueno-koen
Taito-ku
Tokyo 110-0007
JAPAN

FRAGILE
WITH CARE

te: E7480

RN643 **Through Plasa Red** 2007
unique Cibachrome mounted on aluminium and framed
40 × 60 in   102 × 152 cm

FOLLOWING PAGES

RN651 **Through Medium Blue** 2007
unique Cibachrome mounted on aluminium and framed
40 × 60 in   102 × 152 cm

RN644 **Through Dark Amber** 2007
unique Cibachrome mounted on aluminium and framed
40 × 60 in   102 × 152 cm

RN922 **Through Sky Blue** 2009
429 unique luminograms
759 × 155 in   1928 × 394 cm

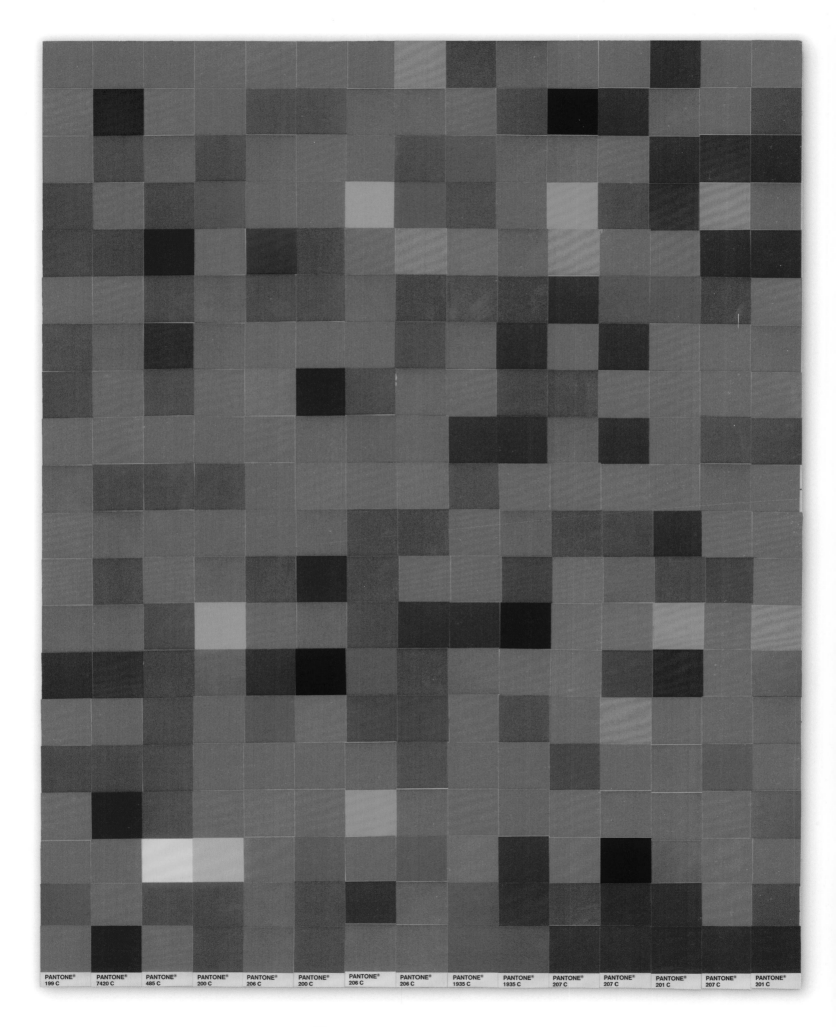

Public Perception of Colour

RN742 **Public Perception of Colour** 2009 DETAIL
self-adhesive Pantone swatches mounted on aluminium
7 parts each 11¾ × 15¾ in 30 × 40 cm

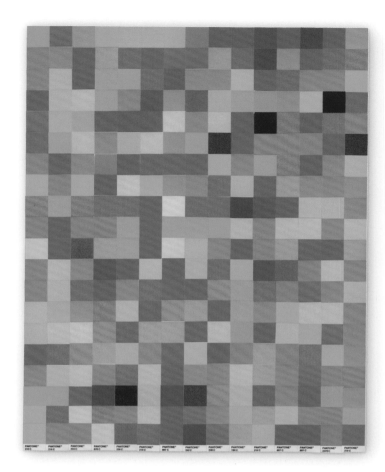

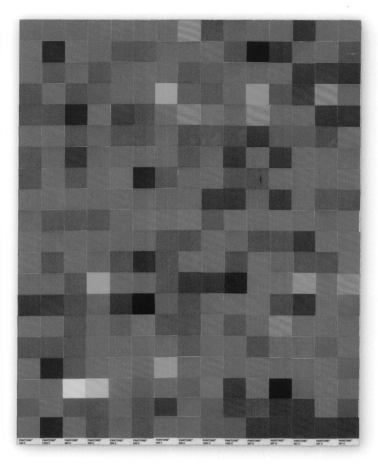

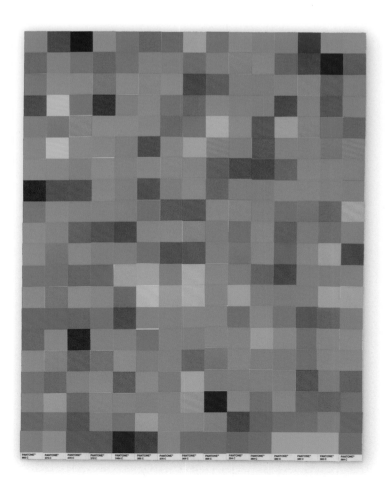

RN742 **Public Perception of Colour**   2009
self-adhesive Pantone swatches mounted on aluminium
7 parts   each 11¾ × 15¾ in   30 × 40 cm

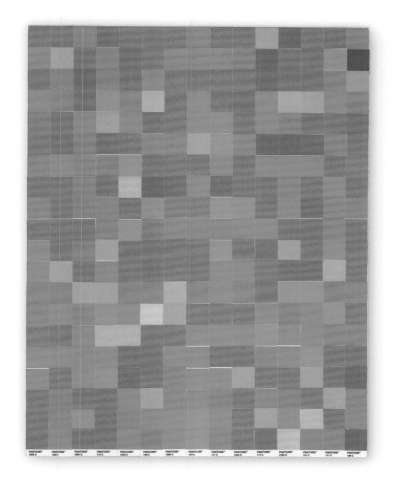
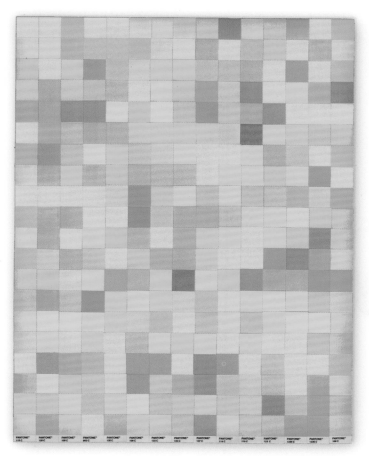
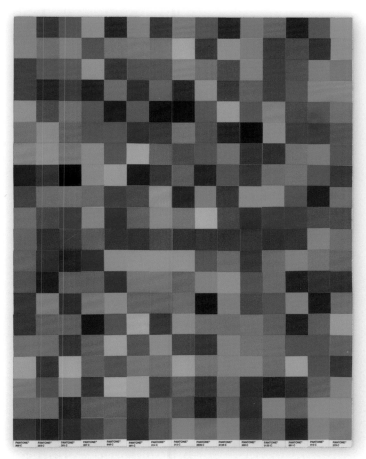

Rob and Nick Carter have never seen the world in black and white. They exist in multiple dimensions – of light, colour and energy. They also work in neon, but their exuberant work is the only sign we need.

Glenda Bailey
Editor in Chief   *Harper's Bazaar*   New York

Paint **Pigment** Photographs

RN876 **Paint Pigment Photograph, Cobalt Blue Medium**   2012
Cibachrome print   Diasec face mounted
42 × 42 in   107 × 107 cm   edition of 5
19 × 19 in   48 × 48 cm   edition of 25

RN869 **Paint Pigment Photograph, Zanderin Golden** 2012
Cibachrome print   Diasec face mounted
42 × 42 in   107 × 107 cm   edition of 5
19 × 19 in   48 × 48 cm   edition of 25

RN866 **Paint Pigment Photograph, Pyrazoquinazolone**   2012
Cibachrome print   Diasec face mounted
42 × 42 in   107 × 107 cm   edition of 5
19 × 19 in   48 × 48 cm   edition of 25

RN881	Titanium White	RN874	Phthalocyanine Green Yellow	RN876	Cobalt Blue Medium	RN865	Napthol Vermillion
RN878	Ultramarine Medium	RN866	Pyrazoquin-azolone	RN870	Dalamar Opaque	RN863	Cobalt Violet
RN867	Flaventhrone	RN877	Cobalt Titanate Blue Red	RN862	Titanium Buff	RN875	Cobalt Bermuda Blue
RN871	Nickel Titanate Yellow	RN864	Transparent Quinacridone Red Blue	RN872	Cobalt Green Yellow	RN879	Dioxazine Violet

Paint Pigment Photographs   2012
Cibachrome prints   Diasec face mounted
42 × 42 in   107 × 107 cm   edition of 5
19 × 19 in   48 × 48 cm   edition of 25

Photograms

RN601 **Cross** 2005
unique Cibachrome mounted on aluminium and framed
17 × 20 in   43 × 51 cm

Photograms

RN601 **Cross** 2005
unique Cibachrome mounted on aluminium and framed
17 × 20 in   43 × 51 cm

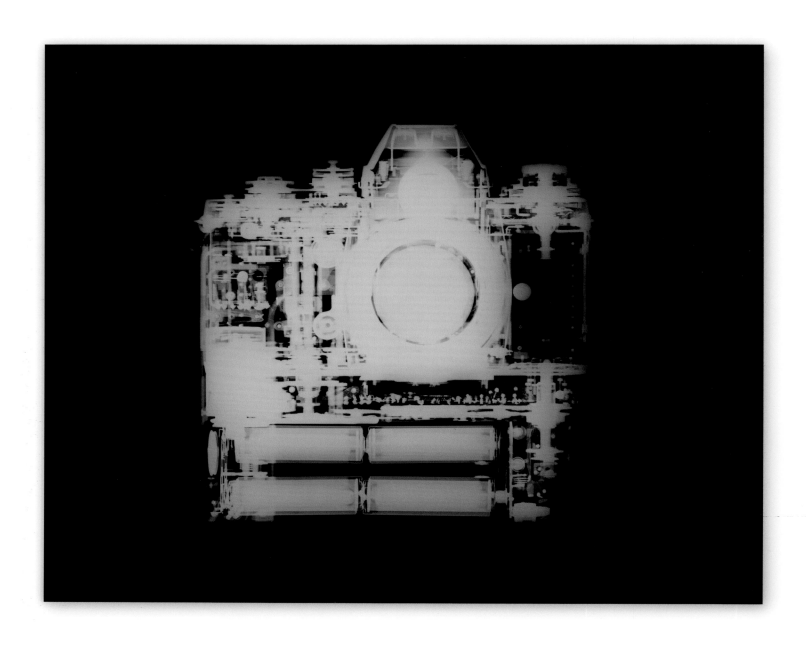

RN885 **Nikon F3 X-ray**   2012
Cibachrome print mounted on aluminium and framed
19 × 17½ in   48 × 44 cm   edition of 12
53 × 46 in   135 × 117 cm   edition of 3

RN883 **Light Bulb**   2012
Cibachrome print mounted on aluminium and framed
15 × 21 in   38 × 53 cm   edition of 12
33 × 46 in   84 × 117 cm   edition of 3

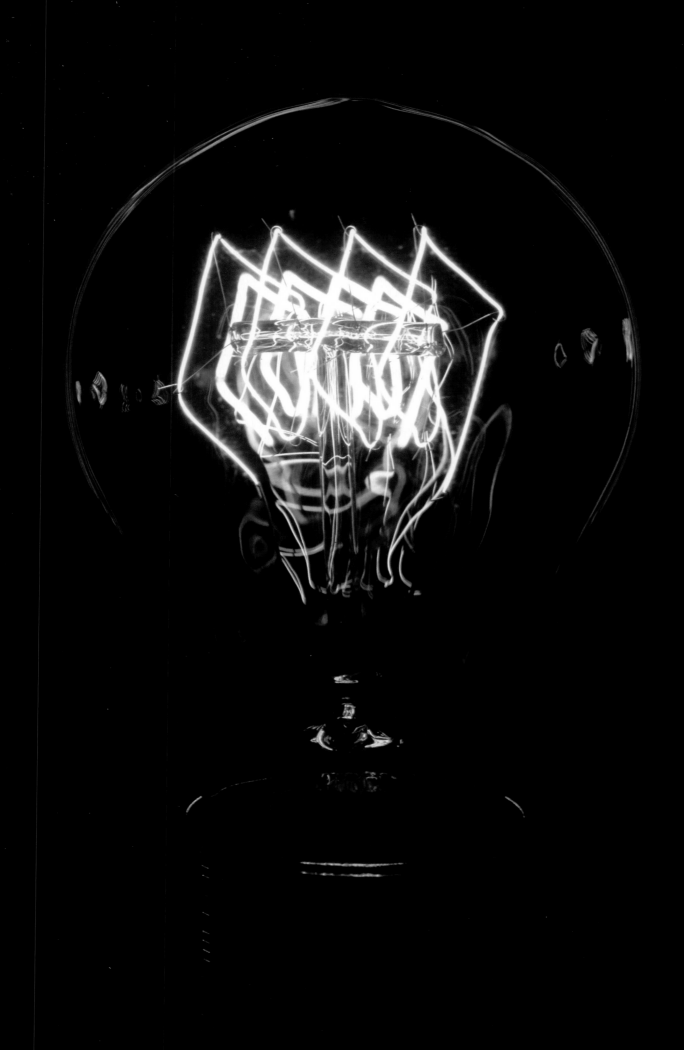

RN662 **Kaleidoscope, Phalaenopsis Orchid** 2007
unique Cibachrome mounted on aluminium and framed behind non reflective glass
36 in ø   91 cm ø

At De Beers we have long been admirers of Rob and
Nick Carter's work and were thrilled when we saw
the **Diamond Photogram**, an authentic and natural
expression of 'The Jeweller of Light'.

Through their incredible cameraless photography
they have revealed the fire, life and brilliance of each
De Beers diamond, and created a uniquely intriguing
and beautiful work of art. We are privileged to have the
Diamond Photogram on display at our flagship store
on Old Bond Street, London.

Francois Delage
CEO   De Beers Diamond Jewellers

Diamond Photograms

RN824 **North Star, Enlarged Diamond Photogram**   2011
Cibachrome print mounted on aluminium and framed
20 × 24 in   51 × 61 cm   edition of 25
35 × 44 in   89 × 112 cm   edition of 5

RN810 **Aquarius**

RN815 **Cancer** RIGHT

RN818 **Libra**

RN811 **Pisces**

RN814 **Gemini**

RN819 **Scorpio**

RN812 **Aries**

RN816 **Leo**

RN820 **Sagittarius**

RN813 **Taurus**

RN817 **Virgo**

RN821 **Capricornus**

Diamond Photograms 2011
Cibachrome prints mounted on aluminium and framed
20 × 24 in   51 × 61 cm
edition of 25

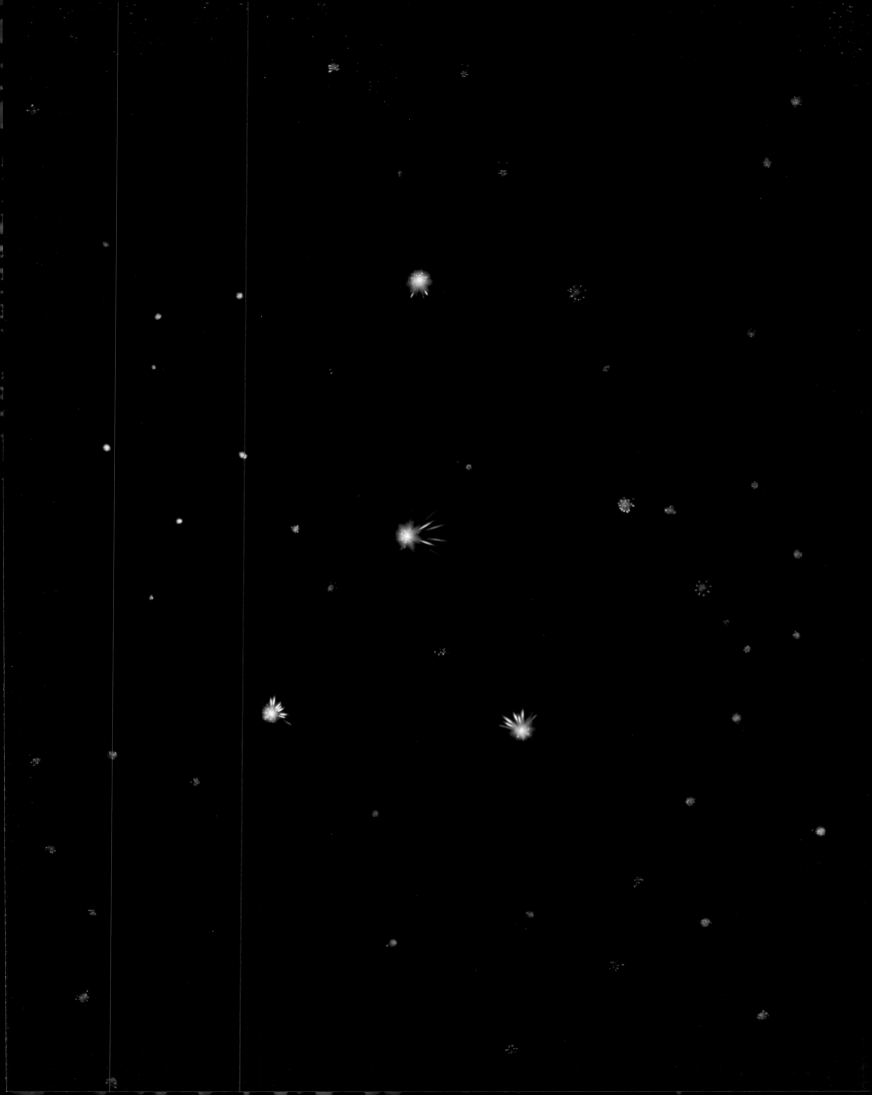

RN431 **Bling, Bling, the imaginary sound that is produced by light reflected from a diamond** 2004
unique Cibachrome mounted on aluminium and framed
54 × 24 in   137 × 61 cm

There are many great artists who work with neon, as well as many who have explored the contextual nature of its appeal. Few, though, have used it with such aplomb as Rob and Nick. In the **Postcards From Vegas** series, they used neon both as a contextual material, and for its contrary qualities. Very simply, they use it as a layering mechanism, making you smile in the process.

My favourite – and the one I bought – is **Hawaiian Surfing**, not just because of its sense of nostalgia, but also because it feels more abstract than some of the others. There is a retro-future aspect to this series of artworks, a sense of fun, and a sense of knowing exactly what works.

I loved Rob and Nick's work long before this series, and they have long since moved on from it, however there is something quite magical about these images, a timelessness and a feeling of genuine exhilaration. Not only that, but I love staring at them. I especially love staring at **Hawaiian Surfing**, although the sensation will not be complete until I finally find the jukebox I'm looking for, having fed it the entire singles collection on *American Graffiti*. This is one picture that should always be accompanied by Booker T. & the MGs' *Green Onions*. Obviously.

Dylan Jones OBE   Editor   *GQ* magazine   Author

Postcards From Vegas

RN783 **Pioneer Pawn**   2011
Cibachrome print mounted on aluminium with neon
41 × 59 × 3 in   103 × 150 × 8 cm
edition of 5   2 artists' proofs

RN808 **Welcome** 2011
Cibachrome print mounted on aluminium with neon
54 × 33 × 3 in   138 × 83 × 8 cm
edition of 5   2 artists' proofs

RN795 **Sunset** 2011
Cibachrome print mounted on aluminium with neon
41 × 26 × 3 in   103 × 66 × 8 cm
edition of 5   2 artists' proofs

RN782 **Holiday Motel**   2011
Cibachrome print mounted on aluminium with neon
67 × 47 × 3 in   170 × 120 × 8 cm
edition of 5   2 artists' proofs

RN790 **Topless** 2011
Cibachrome print mounted on aluminium with neon
39 × 28 × 3 in   100 × 70 × 8 cm
edition of 5   2 artists' proofs

RN798 **Cream** 2011
Cibachrome print mounted on aluminium with neon
62 × 42 × 3 in   158 × 108 × 8 cm
edition of 5   2 artists' proofs

RN797 **Peep Show** 2011
Cibachrome print mounted on aluminium with neon
45 × 29 × 3 in   113 × 76 × 8 cm
edition of 5   2 artists' proofs

RN781 **Blue Swallow** 2011
Cibachrome print mounted on aluminium with neon
59 × 36 × 3 in   150 × 91 × 8 cm
edition of 5   2 artists' proofs

RN785 **Hawaiian Surfing** 2011
Cibachrome print mounted on aluminium with neon
39 × 28 × 3 in 100 × 70 × 8 cm
edition of 5 2 artists' proofs

Paper Photograph Paper

FOLLOWING PAGES

RN964 **Paper Photograph Paper, From Pink to Purple** 2013
framed archival inkjet prints on Hahnemühle 310gsm paper
9 parts   each 10 × 13 in   25 × 33 cm
edition of 12

RN822 **Paper Photograph Paper, White** 2011
framed archival inkjet print on Hahnemühle 310gsm paper
10 × 13 in   25 × 33 cm
edition of 95

RN823 **Paper Photograph Paper, Black** 2011
framed archival inkjet print on Hahnemühle 310gsm paper
10 × 13 in   25 × 33 cm
edition of 95

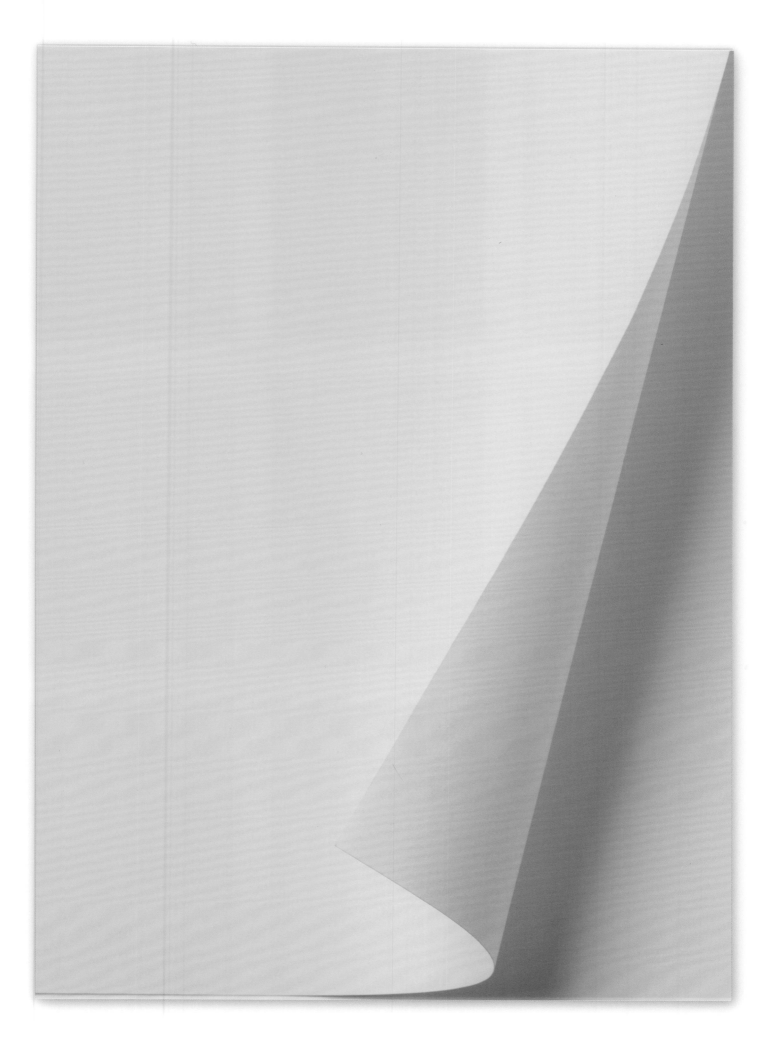

Transforming

I am looking at a painting of a frog lying on its back upon a plinth. But this is no ordinary painting. This painting moves.

As I watch, the frog suddenly twitches into life. Every few seconds another spasm convulses its body, as though someone has just placed an invisible electrode upon its speckled, silvery skin, which glistens with amphibian stickiness. I see it swallow and blink, gasping for air through its upturned mouth like an old man wheezing for his final breath. This stricken frog is alone except for glossy blowflies that begin to circle in anticipation of its impending doom, like hyenas sniffing at weakened prey. There is no way out. With a final heave, the frog arches and locks, its webbed hands and feet reaching for succour that never comes. I am now looking at a painting of a dead frog prostrate upon a plinth.

Except, of course, this isn't a painting at all, but a looped film, lasting three hours, presented on a 21-inch Apple Mac computer screen hidden by a custom-made replica of a wooden Old Master picture frame. This is **Transforming Vanitas Painting**[190] (2012–13) by the married British artists Rob and Nick Carter.

It is not the first 'living' painting that the Carters have made. In 2012, at The European Fine Art Fair in Maastricht, they unveiled **Transforming Still**

Life Painting[178] (2009–12), which animated the famous floral composition **Vase with Flowers in a Window** by the Flemish master Ambrosius Bosschaert (1573–1621), who spent most of his life in the Netherlands, where he shaped the Dutch tradition of flower painting. Over three hours the multifarious bouquet erupting from a vase that Bosschaert had rendered so painstakingly almost four centuries earlier in 1618 was seen subtly to change. The sky, visible through an arched window looking out across a blue-and-green landscape, brightened to a rich cerulean before darkening as time passed from dawn to dusk. The rare and exotic blooms – tulips, roses, marigolds, forget-me-nots, cyclamen, a white trumpet daffodil, amethyst hyacinth, and sundry others – bobbed almost imperceptibly, turning to face the sun and slowly sucking up water which diminished within the vase as the day progressed. A cast of creepy-crawlies entered the scene from stage right and left – bluebottles, ladybirds, butterflies, snails, a caterpillar munching on leaves. Dewdrops at daybreak coalesced upon the petals. Mist in the distance thickened and cleared.

Based upon time-lapse footage recording the fluctuating appearance of real flowers across 24 hours, and created over four labour-intensive years in collaboration with the Oscar-winning creative studio MPC, which produces intricate special effects for feature films and advertisements, the completed work was spellbinding.

The heightened reality of the special effects provided a pleasing modern-day parallel with the hyper-reality of Dutch Golden Age painting. "I nearly cried when MPC showed us the caterpillar moving for the first time," Nick Carter recalls. "It was incredible – I thought, how are they doing this? The answer is that, just like Bosschaert, they were looking at nature – studying real movement, and then transcribing it."

Transforming Still Life Painting proved a critical and commercial success at Maastricht, where one visitor insisted on watching the entire film from start to finish. "A lady in a wheelchair planted herself in front of it and said, 'I'm not moving'," Rob Carter recalls.

For the follow-up, **Transforming Vanitas Painting**, the Carters decided to animate a picture by Ambrosius Bosschaert the Younger (1609-45). Now in the Frits Lugt Collection in Paris, **Dead Frog with Flies** (c.1630), a small oil painting on copper measuring just 5 × 7 inches, is less familiar than the Mauritshuis' oft-reproduced **Vase with Flowers in a Window** by the artist's father. It also offered the Carters greater challenges.

For one thing, the smooth, enamelled perfection of **Vase with Flowers in a Window** had disappeared. Instead, the brushwork was looser, more indeterminate. As a result, it would no longer be enough simply to animate something as realistically as possible, as had

been the case with the flower heads. Now the task was to animate a painting of a thing, so that when its constituent parts were in motion they would not lose their integrity as believable brushstrokes.

Moreover, the sunny appeal of the earlier picture had darkened. Here was a stark image of a frog's cadaver surrounded by four menacing flies. Following through the logic of Bosschaert's picture by animating it, then, meant only one thing – watching this amphibian corpse rot. The point of traditional *vanitas* paintings was to jolt people into reflecting on their own mortality. Yet as the centuries passed, paintings such as **Dead Frog with Flies** lost their capacity to unsettle and provoke. The Carters wanted to revive an old picture so that a contemporary audience would react in a similar fashion to its original viewers. It was a form of pictorial necromancy using twenty-first-century technology. And unlike the pretty flowers swaying gently in the breeze of **Transforming Still Life Painting**, it would be a tough watch.

In truth, I was not prepared for quite how tough it would be when I entered a well-appointed first-floor viewing room in the Fine Art Society on New Bond Street in London to watch **Transforming Vanitas Painting** for the first time. The frog's demise is surprisingly poignant. His death throes induce a sense of sympathy – because he is suffering, we begin to identify with him. "It's like any good film," Rob Carter told me later. "You've got to fall in love with the character that dies otherwise it doesn't work."

The pose reminded me of the foreshortened dead soldier by an anonymous seventeenth-century Italian painter in the National Gallery in London – the two pictures share a similarly sombre palette and mood. When he painted his frog, though, Bosschaert more likely had in mind the traditional medieval and Renaissance theme of the Lamentation of Christ, in which mourners honour the body of Jesus after he has been removed from the cross.

What follows the frog's death in the Carters' film, though, is straight out of a horror movie. The flies lay eggs that hatch inside the corpse into maggots, which in turn feed and grow fat upon the poor frog's innards. We sense their wriggling, unseen presence as ominous bulges ripple and undulate across the animal's bloated belly. Eventually, with the inevitable success of wave after wave of cannon-fodder infantrymen assaulting a stout blockade, they break through – erupting from the abdomen of the frog like the vicious 'chestburster' that explodes from the torso of John Hurt's character in Ridley Scott's 1979 sci-fi horror film Alien.

From this point on, all is carnage. Moving with a dreadful, unstoppable inquisitiveness, the plump, snub-nosed maggots teem across the broken frog like troopers intent on slaughter. One plops then many follow down into the pool of putrefaction that has begun to ooze out from underneath the frog's back. The scene has become a battlefield, as the pillaging maggots lay waste to the frog, razing the citadel of its carcass to the ground. The corpse seems to dissolve before our eyes, as flashes of red, like rivulets of lava, become visible criss-crossing the black wasteland of its interior. The frog's right eye, like a nugget of obsidian, drops to the ground. With wings like rotor blades, flies swoop in and out like Apache attack helicopters supporting the destruction below. Here is warfare worthy of one of Hollywood's classic historical epics.

As the minutes pass, the frog slowly becomes a skeletal wreck surrounded by a squelchy morass of decaying biological matter. The orgy of violence will soon be over, as outlying maggots begin to depart in single file to the left. The transformation of the frog – the transformation of Bosschaert's painting – is complete. I left the Fine Art Society with my mind made up – after I die, I would like my body to be cremated. Nobody who witnesses this unflinching gruesomeness could possibly allow their body to moulder as food for worms below the ground.

Transforming Still Life Painting and **Transforming Vanitas Painting** are two of four 'time-based media' works (as the artists describe them) that the Carters are showing in their major solo exhibition at the Fine Art Society in the autumn of 2013. **Transforming Diptych**[202] presents two films on framed iPads side by side, each one animating a glowing still life of a single piece of luscious fruit flanked by insects atop a cracked plinth, by the eighteenth-century German painter Justus Juncker. Butterflies and other insects flit from one 'painting' to the other, following a flight path randomly generated by sophisticated software designed by MPC. In other words, despite its contemplative calmness, **Transforming Diptych** is infinitely various.

Transforming Nude Painting[212] is more ambitious still – larger than the other three works in the series, and based in part upon footage of a real-life model called Ivory Flame, it brings to life the Venetian painter Giorgione's **Sleeping Venus**, the foundation stone of the tradition of the reclining female nude in Western art. As we watch a beautiful unclothed woman doze, we start to notice her breasts rising and falling in a rhythmic swell. Her eyelids flicker with REM. A gust of soft Italian midsummer air caresses her hair. Occasionally a subtle tremor stirs a hand or a foot. For a single moment, the image matches Giorgione's painting as precisely as possible. "It is important that at one point all of the films resemble the original Old Masters, even if only for a split second," Rob Carter

explains. In the case of **Transforming Vanitas Painting**, this brief instance occurs at frame 5,000 – or 3 minutes and 20 seconds in.

All four works riff on transience, but **Transforming Vanitas Painting** is easily the most grisly of the lot. It is a demanding and uncompromising statement about mortality that refuses to shy away from its difficult subject matter. In a sense, it shares some of its aesthetic with the work of Young British Artists such as Damien Hirst, with whom Nick Carter overlapped when she studied fine art at Goldsmiths in London in the late Eighties. Hirst's important early work **A Thousand Years** (1990) also involves a rotting animal carcass (in his case, a severed bloody cow's head placed inside a glass vitrine), as well as a perpetual cycle of life and death as maggots hatch and turn into flies.

But whereas the effectiveness of **A Thousand Years** relied upon visceral impact, **Transforming Vanitas Painting** does not simply set out to shock. While making it, the artists had to exercise discipline and restraint, so as to avoid letting the artwork lapse into melodrama. "It could have been so corny," says Nick Carter. "Some of the things that we originally thought of – like decaying human heads – were ridiculous. The hardest thing was holding back and trying not to overdo it, to over-animate it. In that way, it is a bit like painting – you have to know when to stop."

As a result, some fairly extreme and troubling material is smuggled into the supposedly civilised world of the Old Masters. Of course, the paintings produced by the Old Masters were often anything but civilised – some of the greatest canvases in the Western canon depict moments of crisis such as murder or rape. But for many people today the art of the past has become remote, perhaps even unintelligible. Rob and Nick Carter want to reverse this trend.

"In our everyday lives we are bombarded with imagery all the time, so this project was about slowing everyone down, slowing down our perception, and making us relook at painting as it was way back then," Nick Carter says. "These days people look at labels in museums longer than the actual paintings." Rob agrees: "When you are seeing so many images on a daily basis, it's harder to get that hit of really good art. We both hope that if the original artists ever came back, they would like what they saw, rather than be horrified by it."

For many people, Rob and Nick Carter's **Transforming** series will offer excitement because of the technical possibilities that it has opened up. Even a few years ago, the technology still did not exist to animate pre-existing paintings to such a sophisticated and believable degree. In this respect, the Carters acknowledge the pioneering and prodigious

efforts of MPC. **Transforming Still Life Painting**, for instance, required several thousand hours of digital rendering – more than a feature-length animated film. For **Transforming Nude Painting** MPC needed 50 terabytes of storage. To put this into some sort of perspective, this is a similar amount required to store 50 hours of standard finished live action feature-film footage. "We met the managing director of MPC Advertising, Graham Bird," Rob Carter says, "and he said, 'You are testing us – but in a good way'."

Yet in order to be successful as works of art, the **Transforming** films must be about more than the technology that was required to produce them – and I believe that they are. **Transforming Vanitas Painting** is not only a spectacular lightshow for people to marvel at, but also a complex, paradoxical work of art. Simultaneously bewitching and brutal, bleak and beautiful, it is a still life in flux – seemingly alive while dramatising the aftermath of death. It employs cutting-edge technology in order to masquerade as something old, and compresses a tumult of drama into the simplest of scenes. Like all of the **Transforming** films, it allows painting to access another dimension altogether: time. The longer you scrutinise these new films, then, the more riddling they become.

Alastair Sooke   July 2013

Transforming Still Life Painting

RN882 **Transforming Still Life Painting**   2009–12
after Ambrosius Bosschaert the Elder   **Vase with Flowers in a Window**   1618
3 hour looped film   computer   frame
23 × 28 × 5 in   58 × 71 × 13 cm
edition of 12   5 artists' proofs

Transforming Still Life Painting is a great gift to the Mauritshuis, which specialises in Dutch and Flemish paintings of the Golden Age, because it offers a fresh perspective on one of the outstanding works in the collection – Ambrosius Bosschaert the Elder's **Vase with Flowers in a Window** (c.1618).

Rob and Nick Carter have literally animated this flower painting, creating an image that moves and changes slowly over the course of three hours. In doing so, they bring out the fragility and transitoriness of the flowers and insects in the original work, and also suggest the passage of time by constantly changing the light cast over the landscape in the background. The care with which the Carters made their film calls attention to the extraordinary quality of Bosschaert's painting.

Transforming Still Life Painting uses a fast medium, but actually has the effect of slowing the viewer down. I have seen people absolutely riveted by this work, taking a great deal of time to watch the still life change before their eyes. This is exactly what we hope that our visitors will do when they encounter the seventeenth-century painting by Bosschaert on which the Carters' film is based – look, look and look again.

Emilie E.S. Gordenker
Director
Royal Picture Gallery   Mauritshuis   The Hague

Being a devotee of the still life genre, in particular the work of Dutch masters, my first reaction to news of Rob and Nick Carter's 'transformation' of one of my favourite works was slight confusion. I wondered how perfection could possibly be improved.

My optimism increased as I recalled a variety of previous works by the Carters. I know their practice to be sophisticated, considered and expertly realised. In viewing **Transforming Still Life Painting** there is no doubt that these artists have executed their first digital painting with a sensitivity that I'm sure the creator of the original work, Ambrosius Bosschaert the Elder, would be thrilled to see.

In what appears a seemingly impossible concept, the artists have brought every aspect of Bosschaert's painting to life. Their reinterpretation of this beautiful work, and its role in our collective cultural *milieu*, has revealed a humanity which is both deeply thought-provoking and visually exquisite. The artists' meticulously executed work honours the inherent beauty of the natural world, while blurring the line between the concept of the reproduction and the original. In what can only be termed an epic, their animated time-lapse film is a result of an artistic, scientific and collaborative approach to the work of an Old Master. The artists took on the role of film directors, working with MPC, to awaken each detail of Bosschaert's stunning painting. They celebrate the perfection of the original, revealing it to new audiences in a contemporary light. Tiny details of the painting now play a more significant role in the composition, to incredible effect.

Rob and Nick Carter have created far from a still life.

Susi Muddiman
Director   Tweed River Art Gallery
Murwillumbah   New South Wales   Australia

Ambrosius Bosschaert the Elder   1573–1621
Vase With Flowers in a Window   1618
oil on panel
18 × 25 in   46 × 64 cm
Mauritshuis   The Hague

I was lucky enough to be one of the first people to see this digitally rendered painting by our friends Rob and Nick. I immediately liked it and my wife Chrissy and I acquired the first in the edition the same day. I sat looking at it for some time before I realised that the time of day was changing. To me it was an older-looking picture − I didn't know anything about it or expect it would move. So it was wonderful when I saw the butterfly land on the flower − I hadn't seen anything like it before; it hadn't occurred to me that a painting could come alive like this. It was the first major piece we have bought for some time − it's marvellous. I have known them since they started out working together. They have always made such clever things.

Sir Peter Blake   Artist

Transforming Still Life Painting was one of the most challenging briefs MPC had ever worked on. At three hours, it was the longest piece of animation we had ever developed. Furthermore, to ensure absolute detail and realism the team studied thousands of hours of nature footage − the task was to capture every subtlety and nuance surrounding events of a 24-hour cycle in the life of a bouquet of flowers. Approached as an animated time-lapse sequence, a huge database of footage was created for every flower in the original painting.

Once the time-lapse flower animation was in place and stretched back to real-time, the creatures were added. From butterflies, ladybirds and flies, to snails and caterpillars eating leaves, MPC modelled and rigged every single component of the painting. Over 45 minutes of creature animation was placed throughout the three-hour piece. The team also added some of the more subtle effects such as dewdrops at dawn, with one dripping down the alcove. The mist in the distance thickens at dawn and then clears for dusk, revealing a distant landscape and even the water level in the vase is animated in 3D.

The end result is an entirely computer-generated animated replica of an original painting − the very first of its kind and paving the way for a completely new genre in the art world.

Jake Mengers
Creative Director 3D Advertising   MPC

Transforming Vanitas Painting

RN915 **Transforming Vanitas Painting** 2012–13
after Ambrosius Bosschaert the Younger **Dead Frog with Flies** c.1630
3 hour looped film   computer   frame
24 × 19 × 3½ in   61 × 48 × 9 cm
edition of 12   5 artists' proofs

MPC's work on **Transforming Vanitas Painting**
fell into three areas. Firstly, creating a frog in various
stages of decay. This was achieved by designing a
number of style frames using in-house concept artists,
which were then mapped to a timeline. To achieve
the transition from the frog's full body to its empty
skeleton, the team used a series of displacement
maps and model changes. These allowed the creation
of varying shapes of decay and, combined with layers
of transparency, enabled the disintegration of the
flesh. The frog animation rig contained the geometry
of a real frog skeleton and once the skin had vanished,
a separate rig allowed the gradual collapse of the
bones to be hand-animated.

A second key component of MPC's work was the
introduction of flies and maggots with believable
behaviour. The creatures were assigned intelligence
attributes and algorithms, such as the ability to avoid
each other and the ability to be attracted to the most
decomposed areas of the skin.

Thirdly, perhaps the greatest challenge within the
work, was enabling the moving piece to retain the
loose painterly style evident in the original painting.
By breaking the painting down into layers, it was
possible to separate the stroke detail from the colour.
Then using a series of camera projections containing
the brushstroke detail, the frog and brushstrokes
moved as one. A very complicated filtering process,
at the 2D compositing stage, allowed refinement of the
brushstroke effect and integration of the layers of 3D.

Jake Mengers
Creative Director 3D Advertising   MPC

Ambrosius Bosschaert the Younger   1609–45
Dead Frog with Flies   c.1630
oil on copper
6⅞ × 4⅞ in   17 × 12 cm
Fondation Custodia   Collection Frits Lugt   Paris

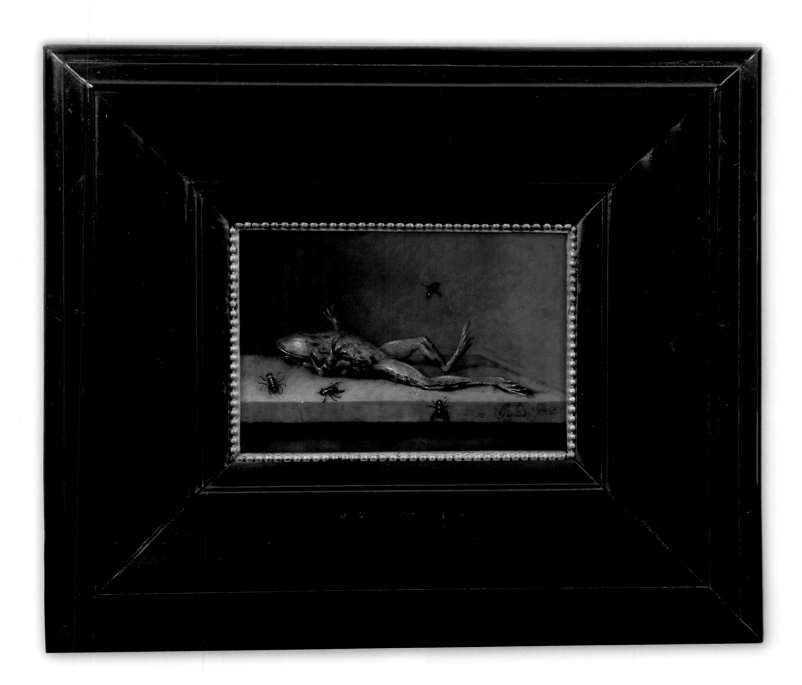

Transforming Diptych

RN918 **Transforming Diptych**   2013
after Justus Juncker   **Still Life with Pear and Insects**   1765
and Justus Juncker   **Still Life with Apple and Insects**   1765
2 works conjoined by random events
framed iPads
each 10½ × 11½ × 1½ in   27 × 29 × 4 cm
edition of 12   5 artists' proofs

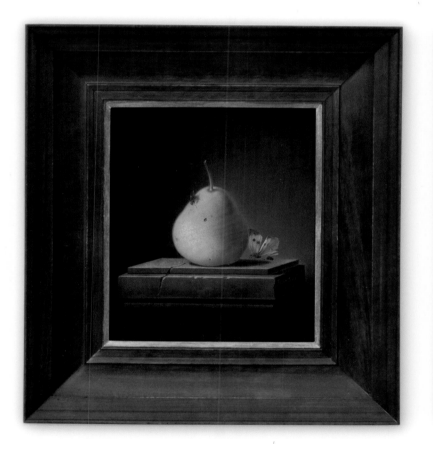

The brief for **Transforming Diptych** was to
create a dual window into a world with a natural
representation of life. To achieve this, MPC digitally
replicated the paintings' environment to provide a static
3D setting and matching light source, while the insects
were brought to life in 3D and their behaviour designed
to mimic reality. The two paintings communicate with
each other, enabling the insects to fly from one piece
to the other, further conjoining the new works.

As well as recreating the fly, wasp and butterfly present
in the original pieces, a ladybird and dragonfly were
also introduced in 3D in the same painterly style of
the original artist. Behind these insects MPC created
a huge database of realistic flight animation sequences.
These sequences are selected randomly, so that
each moment in time containing insect movement
is bespoke. In addition, at indiscriminate intervals,
the pieces match perfectly to the original paintings.

Along with real life flight simulations, each insect
generates a corresponding moving shadow cast over
their environment. To achieve quality in the larger
insects, this involved pre-rendering and pre-treating
both the insects and their shadows for every potential
flight path.

The original paintings were digitally retouched before
being re-projected on to the static 3D environment.
This created separate layers, which enables the insects
to walk or fly realistically around the fruit and create
accurate shadows corresponding to the insects'
proximity to a surface and distance from the light source.

Jake Mengers
Creative Director 3D Advertising   MPC

Justus Juncker   1703–67
Still Life with Pear and Insects   1765
oil on oak panel
8¾ × 10⅜ in   21 × 26 cm
Städel Museum   Frankfurt am Main

Justus Juncker   1703–67
Still Life with Apple and Insects   1765
oil on oak panel
8½ × 10⅜ in   22 × 26 cm
Städel Museum   Frankfurt am Main

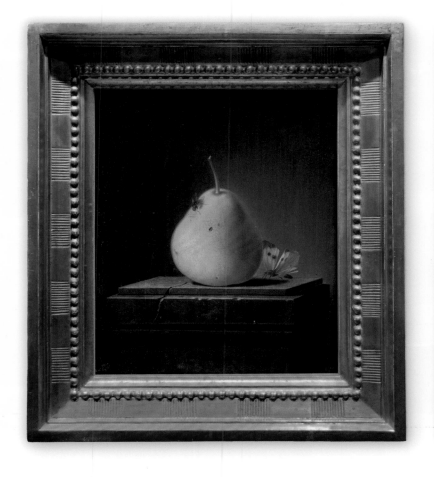

Transforming Nude Painting

RN916 **Transforming Nude Painting**   2013
2½ hour looped film   computer   frame
47 × 32 × 4 in   119 × 81 × 10 cm
edition of 12   5 artists' proofs

Transforming Nude Painting is a groundbreaking piece of art utilising innovative new display technology, which was still in developmental stages at the project's commencement. It also integrates live footage into a 3D painterly environment.

To stay true to the size of the original piece, whilst enduring close-up viewing scrutiny, the team had to employ the use of newly developed 4K/Ultra HD technology. The technology for the two-and-a-half-hour piece had a huge impact on MPC's render farm and storage availability (4K meant working at four times TV standard).

MPC captured hour-long takes of model Ivory Flame 'sleeping', afterwards distorting her body to closely match the painting.

The entire surrounding environment in the new work was then recreated as a 3D model and textured by projecting the painting (with all shadows removed) onto this model. Recreating the sun's path across the sky enabled the team to have changing shadows within the environment that were in line with the light source.

Fur software was adapted to replicate the grass, and a feather system was used for the trees – both were animated to appear to move in the apparent breeze.

Between the changing lighting, moving clouds and movement in the trees and grass, at no time is the background ever static.

Jake Mengers
Creative Director 3D Advertising   MPC

Giorgione (Giorgio Barbarelli da Castelfranco)   c.1478–1510
Sleeping Venus   c.1510
oil on canvas
69 × 42¾ in   175 × 109 cm
Gemäldegalerie Alte Meister   Dresden

Black Tulip

RN914 **Black Tulip** 2012
after Judith Leyster from **Tulip Book** 1643
black-patinated bronze
13 in high 33 cm high
edition of 12 5 artists' proofs

At TEFAF 2012 Rob and Nick Carter presented their film **Transforming Still Life Painting**[178], in which they used digital technology to bring a seventeenth-century flower still life by Ambrosius Bosschaert to life. In 2013 they took everyone by surprise with the sculpture **Black Tulip**, a three-dimensional version of Judith Leyster's 1643 watercolour of the 'Early Brabantsson' tulip.

Black Tulip has become an object of fascination that recalls the glory years of the Haarlem Golden Age (with painters like Frans Hals, Jacob van Ruisdael, Pieter Claesz, Gerrit Berckheyde and Pieter Saenredam), and is at the same time a reminder of the tulip mania that reached its climax in the 1630s, when the prices of exotic tulip bulbs rose to astronomical heights. A single Early Brabantsson bulb fetched 1,010 guilders − an incredible amount of money when you think that in 1642 Rembrandt was paid 1,600 guilders for his **Night Watch**. This bizarre gambling has a good deal in common with the speculative behaviour of banks today. And the total collapse of this tulip mania led to an economic crisis almost identical to the one happening now.

In all its simplicity **Black Tulip** is an image of extremes. Symbolically it is poised between life and death, between earthly beauty and human decay, between artistic ambitions and economic calculation.

Karel Schampers
Director   Frans Hals Museum   Haarlem

Judith Leyster   1609–60
from **Tulip Book**   C.1643
watercolour and silverpoint on vellum
book size   16 × 11 × 2 in   40 × 28 × 5 cm
Frans Hals Museum   Haarlem

Sunflowers

RN919 **Sunflowers** 2012–13
after Vincent van Gogh **Sunflowers** 1888
patinated bronze
23 in high   59 cm high
edition of 12   5 artists' proofs

232

Sunflowers by Rob and Nick Carter is a true fusion of two wildly different but complementary techniques and technologies – one which would be immediately familiar to an Archaic Greek craftsman, the other a truly twenty-first-century technology still in its infancy but with boundless potential. 3D printing, or additive manufacturing, is the starting point of transforming the artists' original to a finished artwork. This modern technology is seamlessly married to the ancient technique of lost-wax bronze casting, over 6,000 years old and relatively unchanged over its history.

The printer used to produce each sunflower head builds the object in a castable wax in layers just 1/50th of a millimetre thick, allowing an utterly faithful and accurate rendering of the artists' vision into three dimensions. No intervention or interpretation by a craftsman is required before preparing the pieces to be cast into bronze. Only very few 3D printers in the UK have the required resolution and accuracy to capture the intricate detail of the artists' original.

Using the product of a twenty-first-century technology, the ancient technique of lost-wax casting transforms the piece into a tactile, enduring artwork. Whilst the principles of bronze casting have remained relatively unchanged throughout history, the most modern equipment is required to maintain the detail in the artists' design. Vacuum investment and computer controlled vacuum casting, allied with the skill and knowledge of master craftsmen allow the integrity of the artwork to be maintained throughout production.

Finally patina is applied to the raw bronze. Many different metal salts, each with its own natural colour, are applied in layers interspersed with heat to control and tame the natural process of oxidation. This gives a lustrous and tactile but naturalistic finish to the piece.

Until very recently this work would be impossible to produce; the limitations of available techniques would prevent the creation of the artists being realised. The technology required to faithfully realise the vision has only just been developed and is only now becoming utilised in the creation of artworks. The piece is an exciting and unique first in the history of casting at Pangolin, one that pushes the boundaries of what is possible to produce in bronze.

Oliver Hale   Project Manager   Pangolin Editions

Vincent van Gogh   1853–90
Sunflowers   1888
oil on canvas
29 × 36 in   73 × 92 cm
National Gallery   London
© The National Gallery   London
Bought by the Courtauld Fund   1924

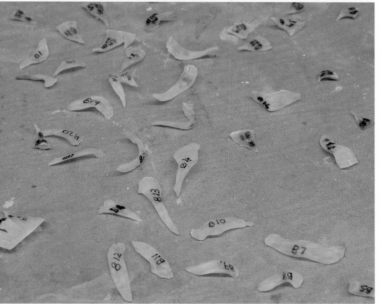

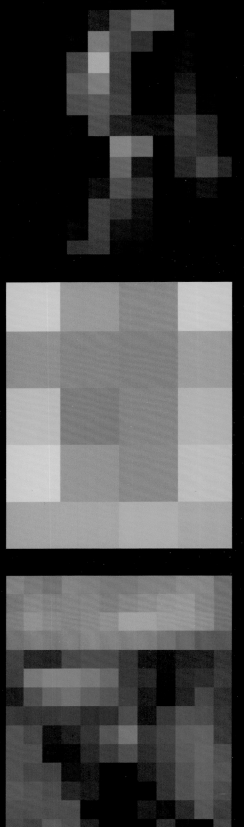
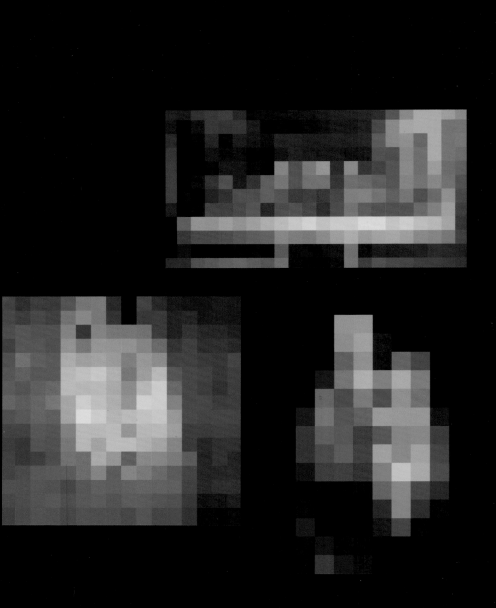

Pixelated Paintings

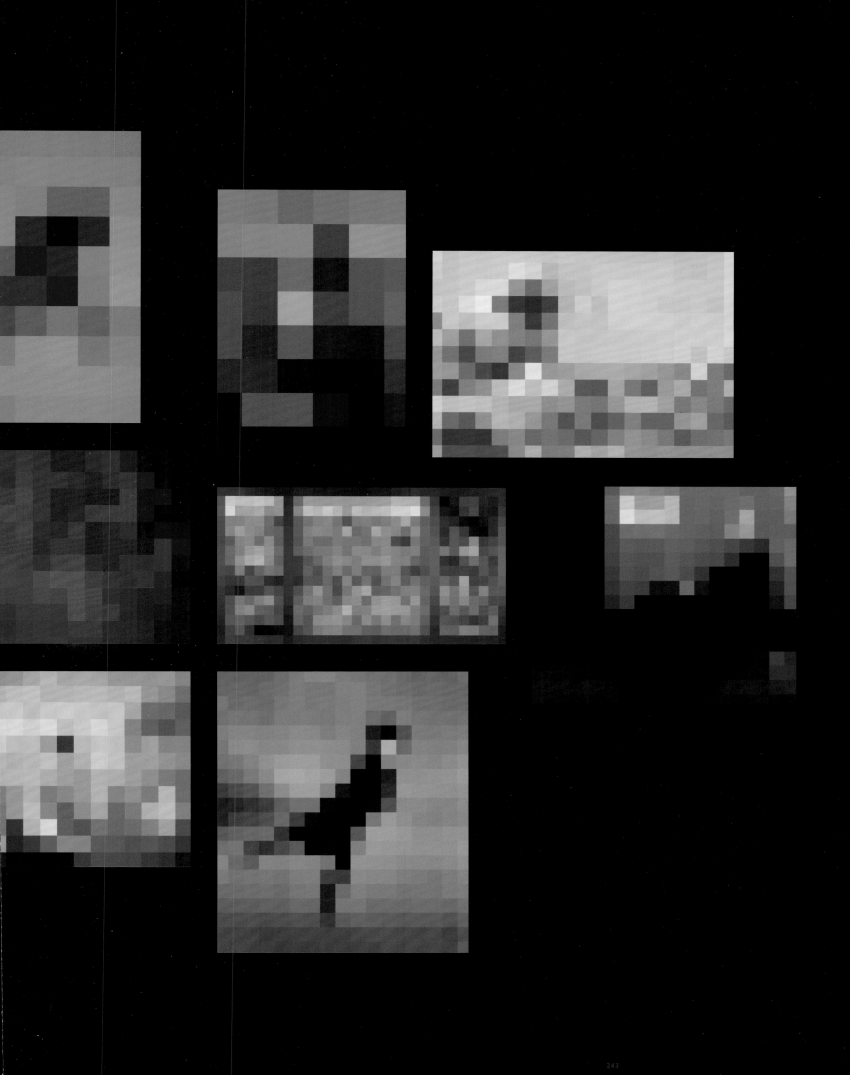

RN910 **1884, Pixelated Painting** 2013
Cibachrome print mounted
on aluminium and framed
24 × 16 in   61 × 41 cm   edition of 12
63 × 42 in   160 × 107 cm   edition of 3

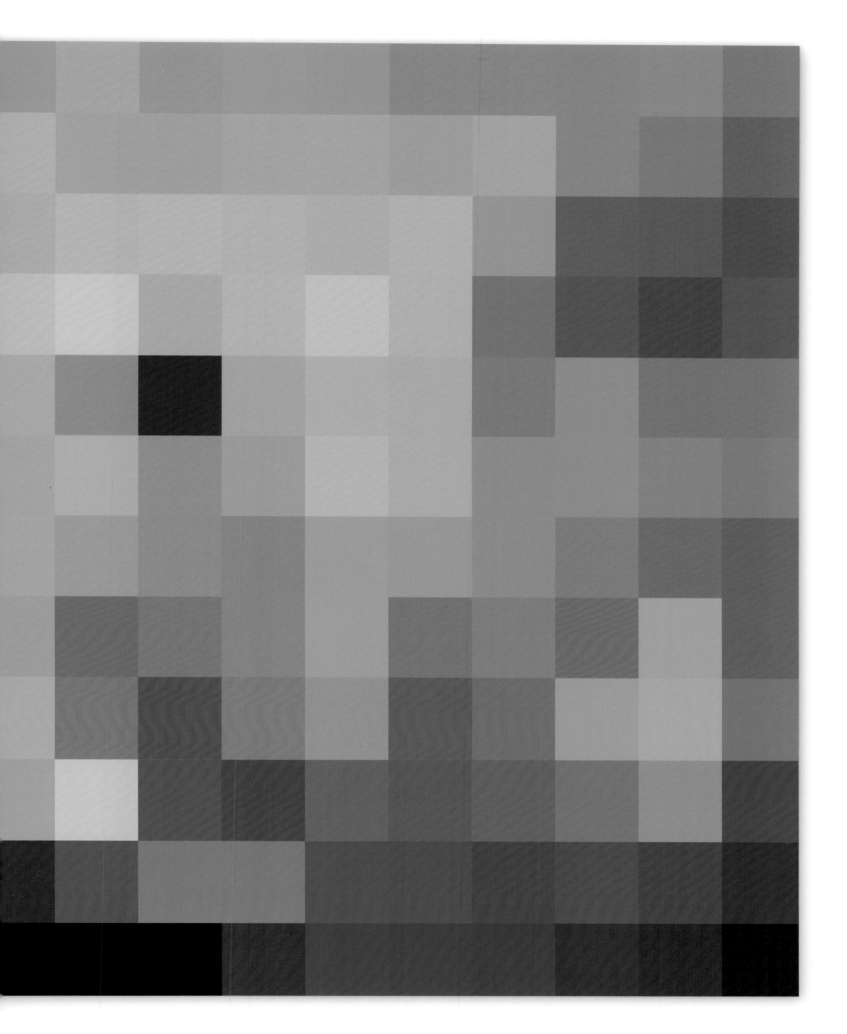

RN900 **1888, Pixelated Painting** 2013
Cibachrome print mounted on aluminium and framed
18 × 22 in   46 × 56 cm   edition of 12
47 × 59 in   119 × 150 cm   edition of 3

Dutch Flowers

Cibachrome prints mounted on aluminium and framed
each 9 × 11 in   23 × 28 cm
edition of 12

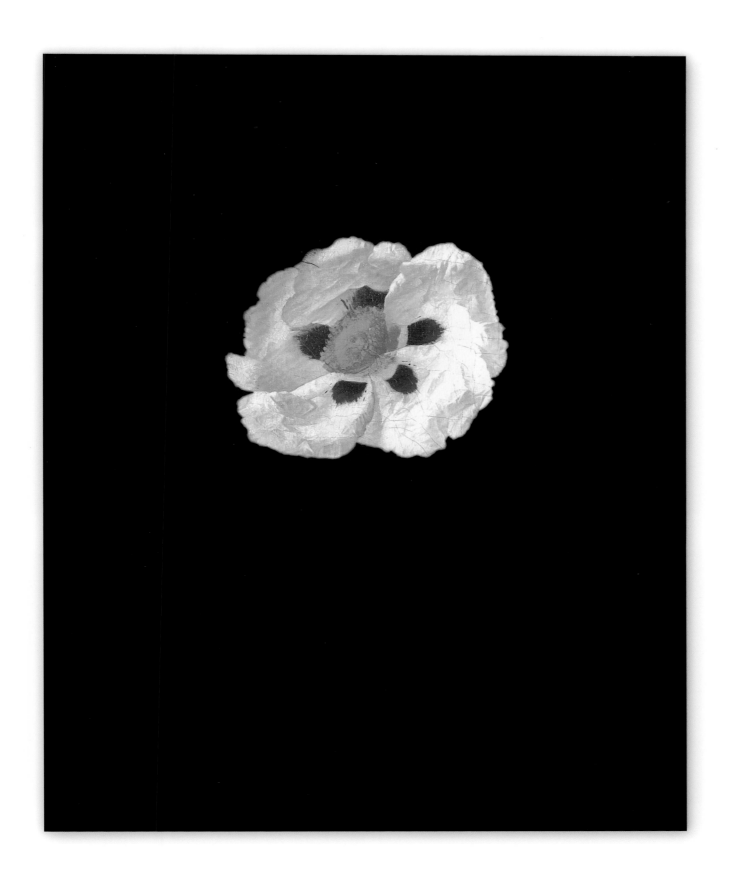

RN943 **Cistus**
after Rachel Ruysch

RN931 Iris I
after Abraham Mignon

RN932 Calendula
after Ambrosius Bosschaert the Elder

RN933 Peony I
after Ambrosius Bosschaert the Elder

RN934 Hyacinth
after Jan van Huysum

RN935 Double Delphinium I
after Jan van Huysum

RN936 Abutilon
after Jan van Huysum

RN937 Calendula II
after Rachel Ruysch

RN938 Peony II
after Rachel Ruysch

RN939 Double Delphinium II
after Jan van Huysum

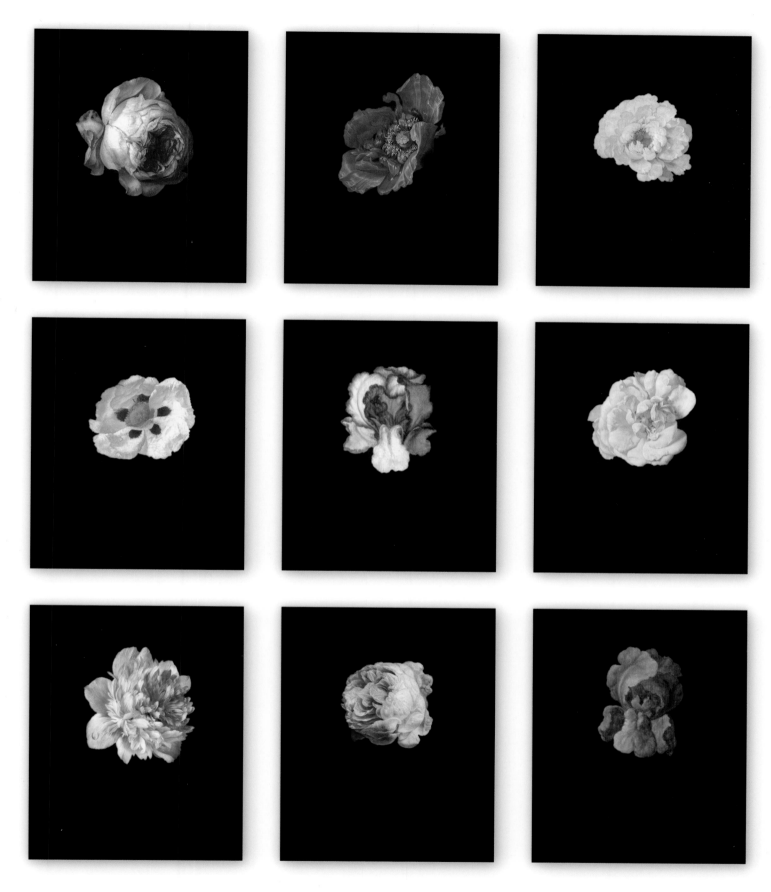

RN940 **Rose I**
after Rachel Ruysch

RN941 **Poppy I**
after Abraham Mignon

RN942 **Peony III**
after Abraham Mignon

RN943 **Cistus**
after Rachel Ruysch

RN944 **Iris II**
after Balthasar van der Ast

RN945 **Peony IV**
after Jan van Huysum

RN946 **Poppy II**
after Jan van Huysum

RN947 **Rose II**
after Theodorus van Brussel

RN948 **Iris III**
after Balthasar van der Ast

RN962 **Dutch Golden Age Collage II**   2013
Cibachrome print mounted on aluminium and framed
20 × 24 in   51 × 61 cm
edition of 12

RN963 **Dutch Golden Age Collage III** 2013
Cibachrome print mounted on aluminium and framed
20 × 24 in 51 × 61 cm
edition of 12

RN922 **Dutch Golden Age Collage I**   2013
Cibachrome print mounted on aluminium and framed
46 × 17 in   117 × 43 cm
edition of 12

Flowers in a Wan-Li Vase

RN899 **Flowers in a Wan-Li Vase** 2013
after Ambrosius Bosschaert the Elder **Flowers in a Wan-Li Vase** 1609–10
Cibachrome prints mounted on aluminium and framed
9 parts each 15 × 20 in 38 × 51 cm
edition of 12

Ambrosius Bosschaert the Elder   1573–1621

Flowers in a Wan-Li Vase   1609–10
oil on copper
20 × 27 in   51 × 69 cm
National Gallery   London

Andy Warhol

Chinese Whispers

RN951 **Chinese Whispers, Signature after Andy Warhol** 2013
30 drawings by 30 different artists   pen on paper   framed
86 × 53 in   218 × 135 cm

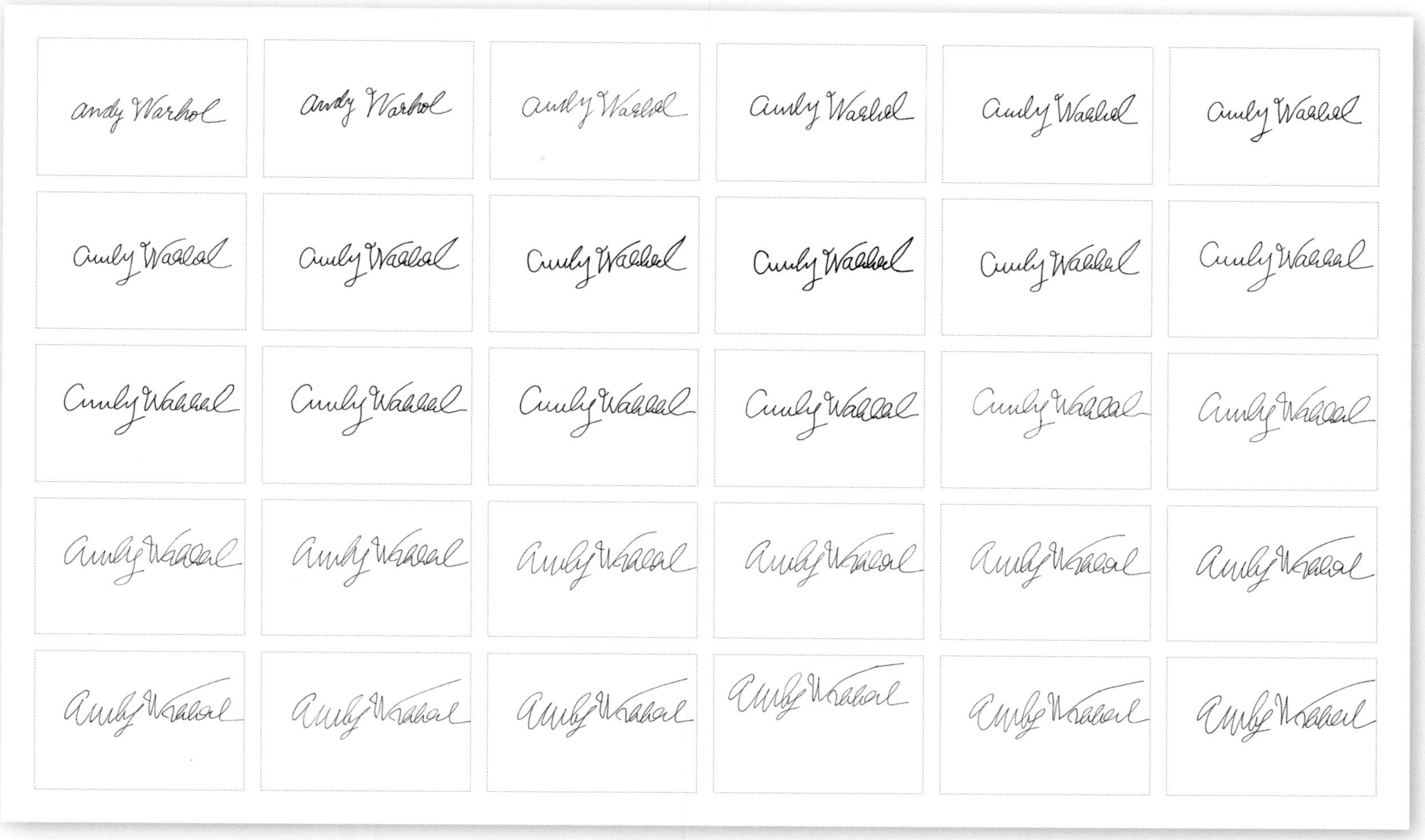
andy Warhol
andy Warhol

Andy Warhol

Mao 1973

RN952 **Chinese Whispers, Mao after Andy Warhol (1973)** 2013
30 drawings by 30 different artists   pen on paper   framed
53 × 86 in   135 × 218 cm

Andy Warhol

Barbie 1986

Andy Warhol

Self Portrait 1986

RN960 **Chinese Whispers, Self Portrait after Andy Warhol (1986)** 2013
30 drawings by 30 different artists   pen on paper   framed
53 × 86 in   135 × 218 cm

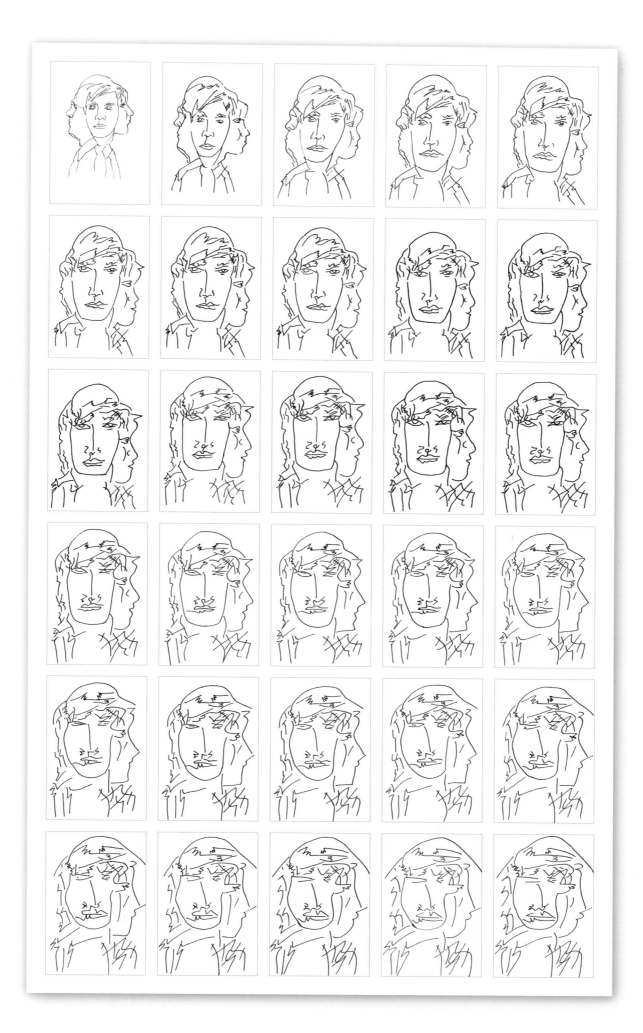

Andy Warhol

Dancer c.1953

RN956 **Chinese Whispers, Dancer I after Andy Warhol (c.1953)** 2013
30 drawings by 30 different artists   pen on paper   framed
53 × 86 in   135 × 218 cm

Andy Warhol

Dancer   c.1953

Andy Warhol

Tulip   c.1955

RN955 **Chinese Whispers, Tulip after Andy Warhol (c.1955)**   2013
30 drawings by 30 different artists   pen on paper   framed
53 × 86 in   135 × 218 cm

Andy Warhol

Coke 1985

RN958 **Chinese Whispers, Coke after Andy Warhol (1985)** 2013
30 drawings by 30 different artists   pen on paper   framed
53 × 86 in   135 × 218 cm

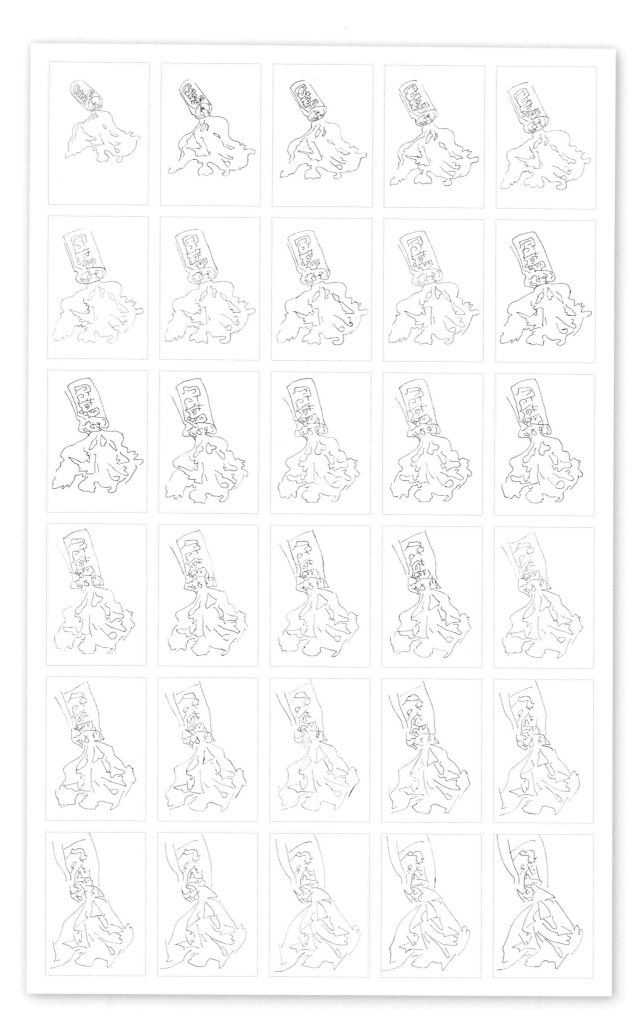

Andy Warhol

After the Party   1979

RN959 **Chinese Whispers, After the Party after Andy Warhol (1979)**   2013
30 drawings by 30 different artists   pen on paper   framed
86 × 53 in   218 × 135 cm

282

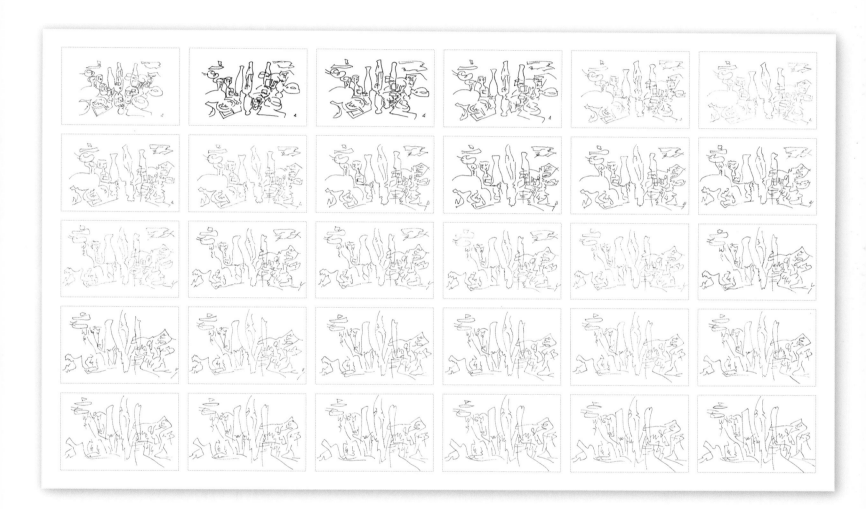

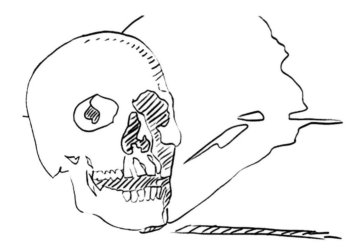

Andy Warhol

Skull 1976

RN949 **Chinese Whispers, Skull I after Andy Warhol (1976)** 2013
30 drawings by 30 different artists   pen on paper   framed
86 × 53 in   218 × 135 cm

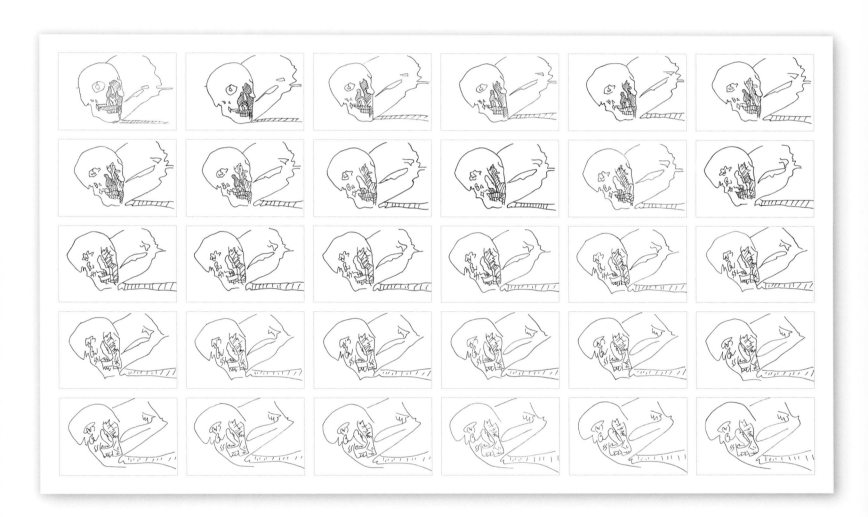

Andy Warhol

Santa Claus   c.1981

RN954   **Chinese Whispers, Santa Claus after Andy Warhol (c.1981)**   2013
30 drawings by 30 different artists   pen on paper   framed
53 × 86 in   135 × 218 cm

Andy Warhol

Dollar Sign   1981

RN953 **Chinese Whispers, Dollar Sign after Andy Warhol (1981)**   2013
30 drawings by 30 different artists   pen on paper   framed
53 × 86 in   135 × 218 cm

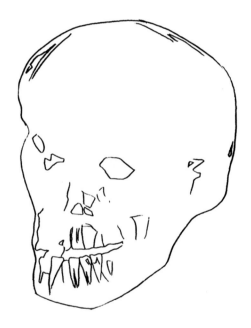

Andy Warhol

Skull 1976

RN950 **Chinese Whispers, Skull II after Andy Warhol (1976)** 2013
30 drawings by 30 different artists   pen on paper   framed
53 × 86 in   135 × 218 cm

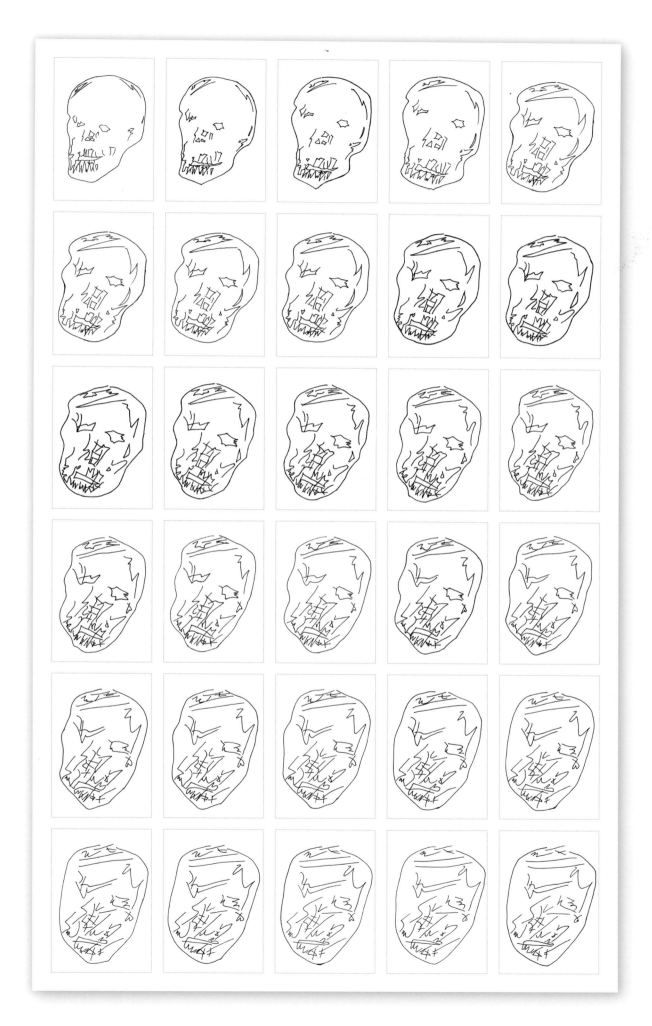

Neon Line Drawings

RN966 **Dancer I, Neon Line Drawing after Andy Warhol (c.1953)** 2013
neon mounted on aluminium
40 × 73 × 4½ in   101 × 185 × 12 cm
edition of 5   2 artists' proofs

RN967 **Dancer II, Neon Line Drawing after Andy Warhol (c.1953)** 2013
neon mounted on aluminium
40 × 73 × 4½ in   101 × 185 × 12 cm
edition of 5   2 artists' proofs

Six Portraits in Six Colours

RN921 **Six Portraits in Six Colours, after Miereveld**   2013   DETAIL
6 Cibachrome prints mounted on aluminium and framed
10 × 12 in   25 × 30 cm
edition of 12

Green, Portrait of a Woman

Composite Portraits

RN974 **Composite Portrait after Vincent van Gogh I** 2013
oil on canvas
24 × 36 in 61 × 91 cm

RN977 **Composite Portrait after Andy Warhol I**   2013
oil on canvas
24 × 36 in   61 × 91 cm

RN978 **Composite Portrait after Andy Warhol II**   2013
oil on canvas
24 × 36 in   61 × 91 cm

Memento Mori

RN965 **Memento Mori** 2013
after Jacques de Gheyn the Elder **Vanitas Still Life** 1603
transparency on surface mirror framed
24 × 26 in 61 × 66 cm
edition of 12

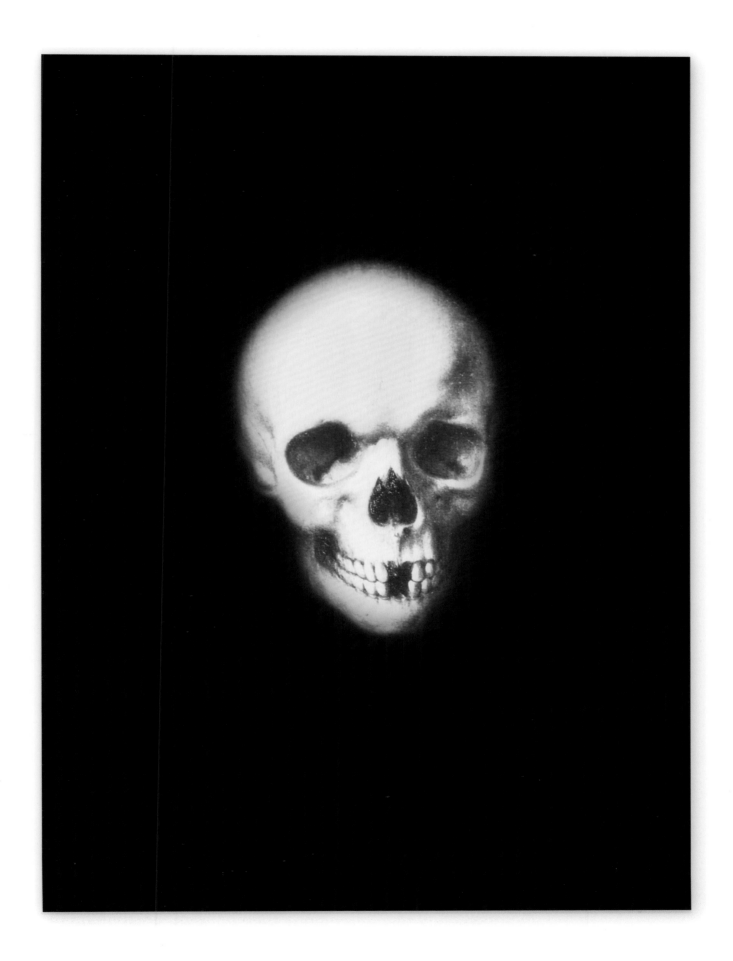

Archive

Grid Pictures

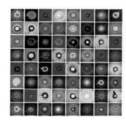

RN113 **Mr Happy Reveller** 2000
unique Cibachrome prints with paint
mounted on paper over board and framed
72 × 72 in   183 × 183 cm

RN74 **Good Times** 2000
unique Cibachrome prints with paint
mounted on paper over board and framed
55 × 55 in   140 × 140 cm

RN27 **Super Jackpot** 2000
unique Cibachrome prints with paint
mounted on paper over board and framed
55 × 55 in   140 × 140 cm

RN64 **De Orbit** 2004
unique Cibachrome with paint
mounted on aluminium and framed
44½ × 44½ in   113 × 113 cm

RN47 **Pressure Drop** 2000
unique Cibachrome with paint
mounted on aluminium and framed
45 × 45 in   114 × 114 cm

Spectrum Circles

RN449 **Full Spectrum
from Magenta to Purple** 2004
unique Cibachrome mounted on aluminium
and framed
41 × 41 in   104 × 104 cm

RN723 **Small Spectrum Circle** 2008
unique Cibachrome mounted on aluminium
and framed
18 × 18 in   46 × 46 cm

RN507 **Small Spectrum Circle** 2004
unique Cibachrome mounted on aluminium
and framed
20 × 20 in   51 × 51 cm

RN724 **Small Spectrum Circle** 2008
unique Cibachrome mounted on aluminium
and framed
18 × 18 in   46 × 46 cm

RN722 **Small Spectrum Circle** 2008
unique Cibachrome mounted on aluminium
and framed
18 × 18 in   46 × 46 cm

RN801 **Spectrum Circle** 2011
unique Cibachrome mounted on aluminium
and framed
49 × 49 in   124 × 124 cm

RN53 **Pulse State** 2000
unique Cibachrome with paint
mounted on aluminium and framed
46 × 46 in   117 × 117 cm

RN148 **Focus** 2001
unique Cibachrome with paint
mounted on aluminium and framed
44 × 44 in   112 × 112 cm

PREVIOUS PAGES AND TITLE PAGES

RN490 **Small Spectrum** 2004 DETAIL
unique Cibachrome mounted on aluminium and framed
34 × 10 in   86 × 25 cm

Vertical Lines

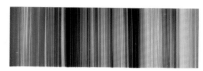

RN709 **Spectrum** 2008
unique Cibachrome mounted on aluminium
and framed
96 × 35 in   244 × 89 cm

RN357 **Vertical Lines, Light and Paint** 2004
unique Cibachrome with paint
mounted on aluminium and framed
38 × 12 in   97 × 30 cm

RN352 **Vertical Lines, Light and Paint** 2004
unique Cibachrome with paint
mounted on aluminium and framed
24 × 24 in   61 × 61 cm

RN123 **Vertical Lines, Light and Paint** 2001
unique Cibachrome with paint
mounted on aluminium and framed
29 × 29 in   74 × 74 cm

RN346 **Small Vertical Lines, Light and Paint**
2004
unique Cibachrome with paint
mounted on aluminium and framed
24 × 12 in   61 × 30 cm

RN432 **Small Vertical Lines, Light and Paint**
2004
unique Cibachrome with paint
mounted on aluminium and framed
24 × 12 in   61 × 30 cm

RN412 **Small Vertical Lines, Light and Paint**
2004
unique Cibachrome with paint
mounted on aluminium and framed
24 × 12 in   61 × 30 cm

Coloured Light Projections

RN753 **Coloured Light Projections** 2006
unique Cibachrome mounted on aluminium
and framed
78 × 37 in   198 × 94 cm

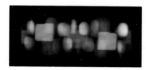

RN639 **Coloured Light Projections** 2006
unique Cibachrome mounted on aluminium
and framed
83 × 41 in   211 × 104 cm

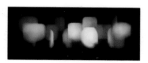

RN609 **Coloured Light Projections** 2005
unique Cibachrome mounted on aluminium
and framed
89 × 38 in   226 × 97 cm

RN529 **Coloured Light Projections** 2005
unique Cibachrome mounted on aluminium
and framed
73 × 24 in   185 × 61 cm

Light Paintings

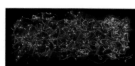

RN22 **Light Painting Blue** 1999
unique Cibachrome with paint
mounted on aluminium and framed
84 × 32 in   213 × 81 cm

RN243 **Light Painting Dragon's Blood Red**
2003
unique Cibachrome with paint
mounted on aluminium and framed
91 × 46 in   231 × 117 cm

Multi-coloured Lines

RN334 **Pink Lines** 2004
unique Cibachrome mounted on aluminium
30 × 60 in   76 × 152 cm

RN428 **Multi-coloured Lines** 2004
unique Cibachrome mounted on aluminium
and framed
71 × 50 in   180 × 127 cm

RN429 **Blue Lines** 2004
unique Cibachrome mounted on aluminium
and framed
77 × 51 in   196 × 130 cm

RN333 **Blue Lines** 2004
unique Cibachrome mounted on aluminium
30 × 60 in   76 × 152 cm

RN335 **Purple Lines** 2004
unique Cibachrome mounted on aluminium
30 × 60 in   76 × 152 cm

Colour Spirals

RN771 **Colour Changing Spiral** 2010
unique Cibachrome mounted on aluminium
and framed
36 × 44 in   91 × 112 cm

RN398 **Colour Changing Spiral** 2004
unique Cibachrome mounted on aluminium
and framed
30 × 37 in   76 × 94 cm

RN383 **Colour Changing Spiral** 2004
unique Cibachrome mounted on aluminium
and framed
32 × 36 in   81 × 91 cm

RN382 **Colour Changing Spiral** 2004
unique Cibachrome mounted on aluminium
and framed
34 × 41 in   86 × 104 cm

RN308 **Colour Changing Spiral** 2003
unique Cibachrome mounted on aluminium
and framed
50 × 60 in   127 × 152 cm

RN472 **Spiral Through Blue** 2004
unique Cibachrome mounted on aluminium
and framed
50 × 58 in   127 × 147 cm

RN374 **Colour Spiral** 2004
unique Cibachrome mounted on aluminium
and framed
45 × 45 in   114 × 114 cm

Light Drawings

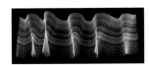

RN174 **Light Drawing Peppermint** 2002
unique Cibachrome mounted on aluminium
and framed
44 × 19 in   112 × 48 cm

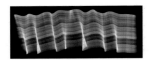

RN151 **Light Drawing Mauve** 2002
unique Cibachrome mounted on aluminium
and framed
94 × 37 in   239 × 94 cm

RN202 **Light Drawing Blue** 2002
unique Cibachrome mounted on aluminium
and framed
96 × 38 in   244 × 97 cm

Neon Landscapes

RN268 **Neon, Clear Red, Blue Glass Coated
Turquoise Pumped Blue** 2003
unique Cibachrome mounted on aluminium
48 × 22 in   122 × 56 cm

RN658 **Neon, Green Glass, Clear Blue** 2007
unique Cibachrome mounted on aluminium
95 × 21½ in   241 × 55 cm

RN661 **Neon, Clear Blue, Bright Blue** 2007
unique Cibachrome mounted on aluminium
89 × 47 in   226 × 119 cm

Mag Lights

RN381 **Mag Light, Multi-Coloured** 2004
unique Cibachrome mounted on aluminium
and framed
45 × 39 in   114 × 99 cm

RN420 **Mag Light, Multi-Coloured** 2004
unique Cibachrome mounted on aluminium
and framed
52 × 46 in   132 × 117 cm

RN430 **Mag Light, Multi-Coloured, Triptych**
2004
3 unique Cibachrome prints mounted on aluminium
each 79 × 47 in   201 × 119 cm

RN425 **Mag Light, Multi-Coloured** 2004
unique Cibachrome mounted on aluminium
and framed
71 × 50 in   180 × 127 cm

Harmonographs

RN622 **Continuous Line Drawing, Harmonograph, VI** 2006
unique Cibachrome mounted on aluminium and framed
36 × 36 in   91 × 91 cm

RN617 **Continuous Line Drawing, Harmonograph, I** 2006
unique Cibachrome mounted on aluminium and framed
36 × 36 in   91 × 91 cm

RN621 **Continuous Line Drawing, Harmonograph, V** 2006
unique Cibachrome mounted on aluminium
36 × 36 in   91 × 91 cm

RN618 **Continuous Line Drawing, Harmonograph, II** 2006
unique Cibachrome mounted on aluminium and framed
36 × 36 in   91 × 91 cm

RN620 **Continuous Line Drawing, Harmonograph, IV** 2006
unique Cibachrome mounted on aluminium and framed
36 × 36 in   91 × 91 cm

RN619 **Continuous Line Drawing, Harmonograph, III** 2006
unique Cibachrome mounted on aluminium and framed
36 × 36 in   91 × 91 cm

Neon Light Works

RN924 **Wavelength** 2006
152 movement-activated neon tubes
71 × 106 in   180 × 270 cm

RN792 **Revolution in Two Parts** 2010
unique double-sided colour changing neon lightboxes
each 98 in ø   250 cm ø

RN754 **Colour Changing Lightbox** 2010
unique Cibachrome transparency backlit with 15 concentric circles of neon
colour changing sequence
fully programmable
52 ø × 6 in   132 ø × 5 cm

RN926 **Wavelength Through Blue** 2009
150 movement-activated neon tubes
590 × 39 in   1500 × 100 cm

RN925 **Wavelength in Three Parts** 2008
3 panels of movement-activated neons
each panel 44½ × 46½ in   113 × 118 cm

RN928 **Read Colours Not Words, From Blue to Orange** 2009
unique multi-coloured neon
118 × 47 × 8 in   300 × 120 × 20 cm

Read Colours Not Words, From Green to Yellow 2009
unique multi-coloured neon
240 × 138 × 8 in   610 × 350 × 20 cm

RN929 **Read Colours Not Words, From Blue to Yellow** 2009
unique multi-coloured neon
69 × 35½ × 4 in   175 × 90 × 10 cm

RN663 **Structural Constellations after Josef Albers** 2007
neon light sculpture
30 × 26 × 2 in   76 × 66 × 5 cm

RN884 **Metropolis** 2012
7 rings of neon
fibreglass moulded egg
30 in high   76 cm high

Orbs

RN760 **Through Blue,
Colour Changing Lightbox** 2010
unique lightbox
3 concentric circles of neon in 3 shades
programmed to slowly fade between
different blues
43 ø × 8½ in   109 ø × 22 cm

RN920 **Orange Orb** 2013
unique Cibachrome mounted on aluminium
and framed
50 × 60 in   127 × 152 cm

RN769 **Blue Orb** 2010
unique Cibachrome mounted on aluminium
and framed
21 × 25 in   53 × 64 cm

Painting Photographs

RN466 **Painting Photograph, Oil** 2004/5
framed Cibachrome print
49 × 59 in   124 × 150 cm
edition of 6

RN457 **Painting Photograph, Oil** 2004/5
framed Cibachrome print
49 × 59 in   124 × 150 cm
edition of 6

RN467 **Painting Photograph, Oil** 2004/5
framed Cibachrome print
49 × 59 in   124 × 150 cm
edition of 6

RN463 **Painting Photograph, Oil** 2004/5
framed Cibachrome print
49 × 59 in   124 × 150 cm
edition of 6

RN456 **Painting Photograph, Oil** 2004/5
framed Cibachrome print
49 × 59 in   124 × 150 cm
edition of 6

RN513 **Small Painting Photograph, Oil** 2005
framed Cibachrome print
18 × 22 in   46 × 56 cm
edition of 6

RN469 **Painting Photograph, Oil** 2004/5
framed Cibachrome print
49 × 59 in   124 × 150 cm
edition of 6

RN458 **Painting Photograph, Oil** 2004/5
framed Cibachrome print
49 × 59 in   124 × 150 cm
edition of 6

Unconscious Paintings

RN894 **Unconscious Painting, TATE** 2012
oil on canvas in perspex case
27 × 33 × 7 in   69 × 83 × 18 cm
posted Friday 29 June 2012
arrived Monday 9 July 2012

RN897 **Unconscious Painting, MOMA** 2012
oil on canvas in perspex case
27 × 33 × 7 in   69 × 83 × 18 cm
posted Friday 29 June 2012
arrived Wednesday 29 August 2012

RN896 **Unconscious Painting, Pompidou**
2012
oil on canvas in perspex case
27 × 33 × 7 in   69 × 83 × 18 cm
posted Friday 29 June 2012
arrived Thursday 16 August 2012

RN895 **Unconscious Painting, LACMA** 2012
oil on canvas in perspex case
27 × 33 × 7 in   69 × 83 × 18 cm
posted Friday 29 June 2012
arrived Monday 17 July 2012

RN898 **Unconscious Painting,
Museum of Western Art, Tokyo** 2012
oil on canvas in perspex case
27 × 33 × 7 in   69 × 83 × 18 cm
posted Friday 29 June 2012
arrived Wednesday 24 September 2012

Luminograms

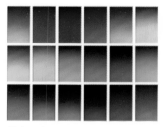

RN775 **18 Luminograms**   2010
18 Cibachrome prints mounted on aluminium and framed
each 12 × 19.5 in   30 × 50 cm
edition of 6

RN643 **Through Plasa Red**   2007
unique Cibachrome mounted on aluminium and framed
40 × 60 in   102 × 152 cm

RN651 **Through Medium Blue**   2007
unique Cibachrome mounted on aluminium and framed
40 × 60 in   102 × 152 cm

RN644 **Through Dark Amber**   2007
unique Cibachrome mounted on aluminium and framed
40 × 60 in   102 × 152 cm

RN922 **Through Sky Blue**   2009
429 unique luminograms
759 × 155 in   1928 × 394 cm

Public Perception of Colour

RN742 **Public Perception of Colour**
2009   self-adhesive Pantone swatches mounted on aluminium
7 parts   each 11¾ × 15¾ in   30 × 40 cm

Paint Pigment Photographs

Paint Pigment Photographs   2012
Cibachrome prints   Diasec face mounted
42 × 42 in   107 × 107 cm   edition of 5
19 × 19 in   48 × 48 cm   edition of 25

RN862 **Titanium Buff**

RN863 **Cobalt Violet**

RN864 **Transparent Quinacridone Red Blue**

RN865 **Napthol Vermillion**

RN866 **Pyrazoquinazolone**

RN867 **Flaventhrone**

RN868 **Benzimidazolone Orange**

RN869 **Zanderin Golden**

RN870 **Dalamar Opaque**

RN871 **Nickel Titanate Yellow**

RN872 Cobalt Green Yellow

RN873 Cobalt Nickel Green

RN874 Phthalocyanine Green Yellow

RN875 Cobalt Bermuda Blue

RN876 Cobalt Blue Medium

RN877 Cobalt Titanate Blue Red

RN878 Ultramarine Medium

RN879 Dioxazine Violet

RN880 Flake White

RN881 Titanium White

Photograms

RN601 **Cross**   2005
unique Cibachrome mounted on aluminium
and framed
17 × 20 in   43 × 51 cm

RN885 **Nikon F3 X-ray**   2012
Cibachrome print mounted on aluminium
and framed
19 × 17½ in   48 × 44 cm   edition of 12
53 × 46 in   135 × 117 cm   edition of 3

RN883 **Light Bulb**   2012
Cibachrome print mounted on aluminium
and framed
15 × 21 in   38 × 53 cm   edition of 12
33 × 46 in   84 × 117 cm   edition of 3

RN662 **Kaleidoscope,
Phalaenopsis Orchid**   2007
unique Cibachrome mounted on aluminium
and framed behind non reflective glass
36 in ø   91 cm ø

Diamond Photograms

RN824 **North Star, Enlarged Diamond
Photogram**   2011
Cibachrome print mounted on aluminium
and framed
20 × 24 in   51 × 61 cm   edition of 25
35 × 44 in   89 × 112 cm   edition of 5

Diamond Photograms   2011
Cibachrome prints mounted on aluminium
and framed
20 × 24 in   51 × 61 cm
edition of 25

RN810 **Aquarius**   RN811 **Pisces**

RN812 **Aries**   RN813 **Taurus**

RN814 **Gemini**   RN815 **Cancer**

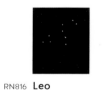

RN816 **Leo**   RN817 **Virgo**

RN818 **Libra**   RN819 **Scorpio**

RN820 **Sagittarius**   RN821 **Capricornus**

RN431 **Bling, Bling, the imaginary sound that
is produced from light reflected by
a diamond**   2004
unique Cibachrome mounted on aluminium
and framed
54 × 24 in   137 × 61 cm

Postcards from Vegas

RN783 **Pioneer Pawn** 2011
Cibachrome print mounted on aluminium
with neon
41 × 59 × 3 in   103 × 150 × 8 cm
edition of 5   2 artists' proofs

RN779 **Sin Will Find You Out** 2011
Cibachrome print mounted on aluminium
with neon
47 × 71 × 3 in   120 × 181 × 8 cm
edition of 5   2 artists' proofs

RN778 **Blue Skies** 2011
Cibachrome print mounted on aluminium
with neon
48 × 77 × 3 in   122 × 196 × 8 cm
edition of 5   2 artists' proofs

RN808 **Welcome** 2011
Cibachrome print mounted on aluminium
with neon
54 × 33 × 3 in   138 × 83 × 8 cm
edition of 5   2 artists' proofs

RN795 **Sunset** 2011
Cibachrome print mounted on aluminium
with neon
41 × 26 × 3 in   103 × 66 × 8 cm
edition of 5   2 artists' proofs

RN782 **Holiday Motel** 2011
Cibachrome print mounted on aluminium
with neon
67 × 47 × 3 in   170 × 120 × 8 cm
edition of 5   2 artists' proofs

RN790 **Topless** 2011
Cibachrome print mounted on aluminium
with neon
39 × 28 × 3 in   100 × 70 × 8 cm
edition of 5   2 artists' proofs

RN798 **Cream** 2011
Cibachrome print mounted on aluminium
with neon
62 × 42 × 3 in   158 × 108 × 8 cm
edition of 5   2 artists' proofs

RN797 **Peep Show** 2011
Cibachrome print mounted on aluminium
with neon
45 × 29 × 3 in   113 × 76 × 8 cm
edition of 5   2 artists' proofs

RN781 **Blue Swallow** 2011
Cibachrome print mounted on aluminium
with neon
59 × 36 × 3 in   150 × 91 × 8 cm
edition of 5   2 artists' proofs

RN785 **Hawaiian Surfing** 2011
Cibachrome print mounted on aluminium
with neon
39 × 28 × 3 in   100 × 70 × 8 cm
edition of 5   2 artists' proofs

Paper Photograph Paper

RN822 **Paper Photograph Paper, White**
RN823 **Paper Photograph Paper, Black**
2011
framed archival inkjet prints
on Hahnemühle 310gsm paper
10 × 13 in   25 × 33 cm
edition of 95

RN964 **Paper Photograph Paper,
From Pink to Purple** 2013
framed archival inkjet prints
on Hahnemühle 310gsm paper
9 parts   each 10 × 13 in   25 × 33 cm
edition of 12

Transforming

Transforming Still Life Painting

RN882 **Transforming Still Life Painting**
2009–12
3 hour looped film   computer   frame
23 × 28 × 5 in   58 × 71 × 13 cm
edition of 12   5 artists' proofs

after

Ambrosius Bosschaert the Elder   1573–1621
Vase with Flowers in a Window   1618
Ambrosius Bosschaert the Elder
oil on panel
18 × 25 in   46 × 64 cm
Mauritshuis   The Hague

Transforming Vanitas Painting

RN915 **Transforming Vanitas Painting**
2012–13
3 hour looped film   computer   frame
24 × 19 × 3½ in   61 × 48 × 9 cm
edition of 12   5 artists' proofs

after

Ambrosius Bosschaert the Younger   1609–45
Dead Frog with Flies   c.1630
oil on copper
6⅞ × 4⅞ in   17 × 12 cm
Fondation Custodia   Collection Frits Lugt   Paris

Transforming Diptych

RN918 **Transforming Diptych**   2013
2 works conjoined by random events
framed iPads
each 10½ × 11½ × 1½ in   27 × 29 × 4 cm
edition of 12   5 artists' proofs

after

Justus Juncker   1703–67
Still Life with Pear and Insects   1765
oil on oak panel
8⅜ × 10⅜ in   21 × 26 cm
Still Life with Apple and Insects   1765
oil on oak panel
8½ × 10⅜ in   22 × 26 cm
Städel Museum   Frankfurt am Main

Transforming Nude Painting

RN916 **Transforming Nude Painting**   2013
2½ hour looped film   computer   frame
47 × 32 × 4 in   119 × 81 × 10 cm
edition of 12   5 artists' proofs

after

Giorgione (Giorgio Barbarelli da Castelfranco)
c.1478–1510
Sleeping Venus   c.1510
oil on canvas
69 × 42¾ in   175 × 109 cm
Gemäldegalerie Alte Meister   Dresden

Black Tulip

RN914 **Black Tulip** 2012
black-patinated bronze
13 in high   33 cm high
edition of 12   5 artists' proofs

after

Judith Leyster   1609–60
from **Tulip Book**   c.1643
watercolour and silverpoint on vellum
book size   16 × 11 × 2 in   40 × 28 × 5 cm
Frans Hals Museum   Haarlem

Sunflowers

RN919 **Sunflowers** 2012–13
patinated bronze
23 in high   59 cm high
edition of 12   5 artists' proofs

after

Vincent van Gogh   1853–90
Sunflowers   1888
oil on canvas
29 × 36 in   73 × 92 cm
National Gallery   London
© The National Gallery   London
Bought by the Courtauld Fund   1924

Pixelated Paintings

RN905 **1907–1908, Pixelated Painting** 2013
Cibachrome print mounted on aluminium
and framed
19 × 19 in   48 × 48 cm   edition of 12
49 × 49 in   124 × 124 cm   edition of 3

after

Gustav Klimt   1862–1918
The Kiss   1907–08
oil and gold leaf on canvas
71 × 71 in   180 × 180 cm
Österreichische Galerie Belvedere   Vienna

RN910 **1884, Pixelated Painting** 2013
Cibachrome print mounted on aluminium
and framed
24 × 16 in   61 × 41 cm   edition of 12
63 × 42 in   160 × 107 cm   edition of 3

after

Georges Seurat   1859–91
Bathers at Asnières   1884
oil on canvas
79 × 118 in   201 × 300 cm
National Gallery   London

RN900 **1888, Pixelated Painting** 2013
Cibachrome print mounted on aluminium
and framed
18 × 22 in   46 × 56 cm   edition of 12
47 × 59 in   119 × 150 cm   edition of 3

after

Vincent van Gogh   1853–90
Sunflowers   1888
oil on canvas
36 × 29 in   91 × 74 cm
National Gallery   London

RN907 **1665, Pixelated Painting** 2013
Cibachrome print mounted on aluminium
and framed
16 × 22 in   41 × 58 cm   edition of 12
43 × 60 in   109 × 152 cm   edition of 3

after

Johannes Vermeer   1632–75
Girl with a Pearl Earring   1665
oil on canvas
15 × 17 in   38 × 43 cm
Mauritshuis   The Hague

RN903 **1762, Pixelated Painting** 2013
Cibachrome print mounted on aluminium
and framed
20 × 24 in   51 × 61 cm   edition of 12
49 × 59 in   124 × 150 cm   edition of 3

after

George Stubbs   1724–1806
Whistlejacket   1762
oil on canvas
97 × 115 in   246 × 292 cm
National Gallery   London

RN904 **1495–1498, Pixelated Painting** 2013
Cibachrome print mounted on aluminium
and framed
24 × 13 in   61 × 33 cm   edition of 12
64 × 34 in   163 × 86 cm   edition of 3

after

Leonardo da Vinci   1452–1519
The Last Supper   1495–98
tempera and mixed media on plaster
181 × 346 in   460 × 879 cm
Santa Maria delle Grazie   Milan

RN912 **1505, Pixelated Painting** 2013
Cibachrome print mounted on aluminium
and framed
15 × 23 in   38 × 58 cm   edition of 12
41 × 63 in   104 × 160 cm   edition of 3

after

Raphael   1452–1519
Madonna del Granduca   1505
oil on wood
22 × 33 in   56 × 85 cm
Palazzo Pitti   Florence

RN906 **1893, Pixelated Painting** 2013
Cibachrome print mounted on aluminium
and framed
18 × 22 in   46 × 58 cm   edition of 12
49 × 62 in   124 × 157 cm   edition of 3

after

Edvard Munch   1863–1944
The Scream   1893
oil, tempera and pastel on cardboard
29 × 36 in   155 × 124 cm
National Gallery   Oslo

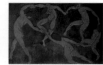

RN909 **1910, Pixelated Painting** 2013
Cibachrome print mounted on aluminium
and framed
24 × 16 in 61 × 41 cm edition of 12
64 × 43 in 163 × 109 cm edition of 3
after

Henri Matisse 1869–1954
Dance 1910
oil on canvas
154 × 102 in 391 × 259 cm
The Hermitage St. Petersburg

RN902 **1503–1519, Pixelated Painting** 2013
Cibachrome print mounted on aluminium
and framed
15 × 22 in 38 × 56 cm edition of 12
45 × 53 in 114 × 135 cm edition of 3
after

Leonardo da Vinci 1452–1519
Mona Lisa 1503–19
oil on poplar
21 × 30 in 150 × 102 cm
Musée du Louvre Paris

RN901 **1480–1505, Pixelated Painting** 2013
Cibachrome print mounted on aluminium
and framed
23 × 13 in 58 × 33 cm edition of 12
64 × 34 in 163 × 86 cm edition of 3
after

Hieronymus Bosch 1450–1516
The Garden of Earthly Delights 1480–1505
oil on panel
154 × 87 in 391 × 221 cm
Museo del Prado Madrid

RN913 **1790, Pixelated Painting** 2013
Cibachrome print mounted on aluminium
and framed
20 × 23 in 51 × 58 cm edition of 12
49 × 57 in 124 × 145 cm edition of 3
after

Henry Raeburn 1756–1823
**The Reverend Robert Walker Skating on
Duddingston Lock** 1790
oil on canvas
10 × 12 in 25 × 30 cm
National Gallery of Scotland Edinburgh

RN908 **1829–1832, Pixelated Painting** 2013
Cibachrome print mounted on aluminium
and framed
24 × 17 in 61 × 43 cm edition of 12
64 × 44 in 163 × 112 cm edition of 3
after

Katsushika Hokusai 1760–1849
The Great Wave off Kanagawa 1829–32
woodblock print
15 × 10 in 38 × 25 cm
Metropolitan Museum of Modern Art New York

RN911 **1871, Pixelated Painting** 2013
Cibachrome print mounted on aluminium
and framed
21 × 18 in 53 × 46 cm edition of 12
56 × 49 in 142 × 124 cm edition of 3
after

James McNeill Whistler 1834–1903
Arrangement in Grey and Black No.1 1871
oil on canvas
64 × 57 in 163 × 145 cm
Musée d'Orsay Paris

Dutch Flowers

2013
Cibachrome prints mounted on aluminium
and framed
each 9 × 11 in 23 × 28 cm
edition of 12

RN931 **Iris I after Abraham Mignon**
RN941 **Poppy I after Abraham Mignon**
RN942 **Peony III after Abraham Mignon**

after

Abraham Mignon 1640–79
Still Life with Flowers and a Watch c.1660–79
oil on canvas 24 × 29½ in 60 × 75 cm
Rijksmuseum Amsterdam

RN932 **Calendula I
after Ambrosius Bosschaert the Elder**

RN933 **Peony I
after Ambrosius Bosschaert the Elder**

after

Ambrosius Bosschaert the Elder 1573–1621
Flowers in a Glass Vase 1614
oil on copper 8 × 10 in 21 × 26 cm
National Gallery London

RN936 **Abutilon after Jan van Huysum**

after

Jan van Huysum 1682–1749
Hollyhocks and other Flowers in a Vase 1702–20
oil on canvas 20 × 24 in 52 × 62 cm
National Gallery London

RN934 Hyacinth after Jan van Huysum

RN935 Double Delphiunium I
after Jan van Huysum

RN939 Double Delphinium II
after Jan van Huysum

RN945 Peony IV after Jan van Huysum

RN946 Poppy II after Jan van Huysum

after

Jan van Huysum   1682–1749
Vase of Flowers   1722
oil on panel   24 × 31 in   61 × 79 cm
Getty Museum   Los Angeles

RN937 Calendula II after Rachel Ruysch

RN940 Rose I after Rachel Ruysch

RN943 Cistus after Rachel Ruysch

after

Rachel Ruysch   1664–1750
Still Life with Flowers on a Marble Tabletop   1716
oil on canvas   15½ × 19 in   40 × 49 cm
Rijksmuseum   Amsterdam

RN938 Peony II after Rachel Ruysch

after

Rachel Ruysch   1664–1750
Flowers in a Vase   c.1685
oil on canvas   17 × 22 in   43 × 57 cm
National Gallery   London

RN944 Iris II after Balthasar van der Ast

RN948 Iris III after Balthasar van der Ast

after

Balthasar van der Ast   1593–1657
Still Life with Flowers   c.1625–30
oil on panel   17 × 23 in   43 × 59 cm
Rijksmuseum   Amsterdam

RN947 Rose II
after Paulus Theodorus van Brussel

after

Paulus Theodorus van Brussel   1754–95
Flowers in a Vase   1792
oil on mahogany   24 × 31 in   61 × 78 cm
National Gallery   London

RN922 **Dutch Golden Age Collage I**   2013
Cibachrome print mounted on aluminium
and framed
46 × 17 in   117 × 43 cm   edition of 12
ALSO ON ENDPAPERS

RN962 **Dutch Golden Age Collage II**   2013
RN963 **Dutch Golden Age Collage III**   2013
Cibachrome prints mounted on aluminium
and framed
20 × 24 in   51 × 61 cm   edition of 12

Flowers in a Wan-Li Vase

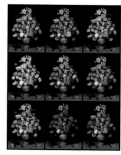

RN899 **Flowers in a Wan-Li Vase**   2013
Cibachrome prints mounted on aluminium
and framed
9 parts   each 15 × 20 in   38 × 51 cm
edition of 12

after

Ambrosius Bosschaert the Elder   1573–1621
Flowers in a Wan-Li Vase   1609–10
oil on copper
20 × 27 in   51 × 69 cm
National Gallery   London

Chinese Whispers

RN951 **Chinese Whispers,
Signature after Andy Warhol**   2013
30 drawings by 30 different artists
pen on paper   framed
86 × 53 in   218 × 135 cm

RN952 **Chinese Whispers,
Mao after Andy Warhol (1973)**   2013
30 drawings by 30 different artists
pen on paper   framed
53 × 86 in   135 × 218 cm

RN961 **Chinese Whispers,
Barbie after Andy Warhol (1986)**
2013
30 drawings by 30 different artists
pen on paper   framed
53 × 86 in   135 × 218 cm

RN960 **Chinese Whispers,**
Self Portrait after Andy Warhol (1986)
2013
30 drawings by 30 different artists
pen on paper   framed
53 × 86 in   135 × 218 cm

RN956 **Chinese Whispers,**
Dancer I after Andy Warhol (c.1953)
2013
30 drawings by 30 different artists
pen on paper   framed
53 × 86 in   135 × 218 cm

RN957 **Chinese Whispers,**
Dancer II after Andy Warhol (c.1953)
2013
30 drawings by 30 different artists
pen on paper   framed
53 × 86 in   135 × 218 cm

RN955 **Chinese Whispers,**
Tulip after Andy Warhol (c.1955)
2013
30 drawings by 30 different artists
pen on paper   framed
53 × 86 in   135 × 218 cm

RN958 **Chinese Whispers,**
Coke after Andy Warhol (1985)   2013
30 drawings by 30 different artists
pen on paper   framed
53 × 86 in   135 × 218 cm

RN959 **Chinese Whispers,**
After the Party after Andy Warhol
(1979)   2013
30 drawings by 30 different artists
pen on paper   framed
86 × 53 in   218 × 135 cm

RN949 **Chinese Whispers,**
Skull I after Andy Warhol (1976)   2013
30 drawings by 30 different artists
pen on paper   framed
53 × 86 in   135 × 218 cm

RN954 **Chinese Whispers,**
Santa Claus after Andy Warhol
(c.1981)   2013
30 drawings by 30 different artists
pen on paper   framed
53 × 86 in   135 × 218 cm

RN953 **Chinese Whispers,**
Dollar Sign after Andy Warhol (1981)
2013
30 drawings by 30 different artists
pen on paper   framed
53 × 86 in   135 × 218 cm

RN950 **Chinese Whispers,**
Skull II after Andy Warhol (1976)   2013
30 drawings by 30 different artists
pen on paper   framed
86 × 53 in   218 × 135 cm

Neon Line Drawings

RN966 **Dancer I, Neon Line Drawing**
after Andy Warhol (c.1953)   2013
neon mounted on aluminium
40 × 73 × 4½ in   101 × 185 × 12 cm
edition of 5   2 artists' proofs

RN967 **Dancer II, Neon Line Drawing**
after Andy Warhol (c.1953)   2013
neon mounted on aluminium
40 × 73 × 4½ in   101 × 185 × 12 cm
edition of 5   2 artists' proofs

Six Portraits in Six Colours

RN921 **Six Portraits in Six Colours,**
after Miereveld   2013
6 Cibachrome prints mounted on aluminium
and framed
10 × 12 in   25 × 30 cm
edition of 12

Pink, Portrait of a Woman

after

Michiel Jansz van Miereveld   1567–1641
Portrait of a Woman   1618
oil on oak
20 × 24⅜ in   51 × 62 cm
National Gallery   London

Orange, Portrait of a Woman
with a Lace Collar

after

Michiel Jansz van Miereveld   1567–1641
Portrait of a Woman with a Lace Collar   1632–35
oil on wood
23⅝ × 29 in   60 × 75 cm
Metropolitan Museum of Art   New York

Yellow, Margaretha van Clootwijk,
Wife of Jacob van Dalen

after

Michiel Jansz van Miereveld   1567–1641
Margaretha van Clootwijk,
Wife of Jacob van Dalen   1632–39
oil on wood
27½ × 28 in   58 × 71 cm
Metropolitan Museum of Art   New York

after

Green, Portrait of a Woman

Michiel Jansz van Miereveld   1567–1641
Portrait of a Woman   1625
oil on wood
Musée des Beaux-Arts de Lyon

Blue, Elizabeth, Queen of Bohemia

after

Michiel Jansz van Miereveld   1567–1641
Elizabeth, Queen of Bohemia   c.1623
oil on panel
23⅝ × 27½ in   60 × 70 cm
National Gallery   London

Purple, Portrait of a Young Woman

after

Michiel Jansz van Miereveld   1567–1641
Portrait of a Young Woman   1630
oil on panel
27½ × 28¾ in   58 × 70 cm
Kunsthistorisches Museum   Vienna

Composite Portraits

RN974 **Composite Portrait after Vincent van Gogh I** 2013
oil on canvas
24 × 36 in   61 × 91 cm
after

Vincent van Gogh   1853–90
Self Portrait   1887
Self Portrait   1887
Self Portrait   1889
Self Portrait   1889
Self Portrait with Palette   1889

RN973 **Composite Portrait after Anthony van Dyck** 2013
oil on canvas
24 × 36 in   61 × 91 cm
after

Anthony van Dyck   1599–1641
Richard Boyle, 1st Earl of Burlington and 2nd Earl of Cork
William II and his wife Mary Stuart (detail)   1641
Philip Herbert, 4th Earl of Pembroke
The Artist Marten Pepijn   c.1506
Inigo Jones   1632–33

RN970 **Composite Portrait after Raphael** 2013
oil on canvas
24 × 36 in   61 × 91 cm
after

Raphael (Raffaello Sanzio da Urbino)   1483–1520
St. Sebastian   c.1501–2
Maddalena Doni   1506
Elisabetta Gonzaga   1504–5
Guidobaldo da Montefeltro, Duke of Urbino   c.1506
Man Holding and Apple   1500
Maddalena Doni   1506

RN977 **Composite Portrait after Andy Warhol I** 2013
oil on canvas
24 × 36 in   61 × 91 cm
after

Andy Warhol   1928–87
Turquoise Marilyn   1964
Debbie Harry   1980
Liza Minelli   c.1978
Red Jackie   1964
Caroline Herrera   1979

RN978 **Composite Portrait after Andy Warhol II** 2013
oil on canvas
24 × 36 in   61 × 91 cm
after

Andy Warhol   1928–87
Portrait of Joseph Beuys   1980
Michael Jackson   1984
Erich Marx   1978
Franz Kafka (from Ten Portraits of Jews of the Twentieth Century)   1980
Mao   1973

RN971 **Composite Portrait after Rembrandt Harmenszoon van Rijn** 2013
oil on canvas
24 × 36 in   61 × 91 cm
after

Rembrandt Harmenszoon van Rijn   1606–69
Self Portrait   1663
Self Portrait as the Apostle Paul   1661
Self Portrait at an Early Age   1629
Self Portrait with Velvet Cap and a Coat with Fur Collar   1634

RN968 **Composite Portrait after Albrecht Dürer** 2013
oil on canvas
24 × 36 in   61 × 91 cm
after

Albrecht Dürer   1471–1528
Albrecht Dürer the Elder   1490
Jacob Muffle   1526
Hieronymus Holzschuher   1526
Albrecht Dürer's Father   1497
A Cleric   1516
Bernhard von Reesen   1521

RN969 **Composite Portrait after Michiel Jansz van Miereveld** 2013
oil on canvas
24 × 36 in   61 × 91 cm
after

Michiel Jansz van Miereveld   1567–1641
Anne, Lady Carleton   c.1625
A Lady
A Woman
Corvina Hezebroek van Hofdijck   1618
Margaretha van Clootwijk, Wife of Jacob van Dalen   1639
A Cleric   1516
Elizabeth, Queen of Bohemia   c.1623

RN972 **Composite Portrait after Titian** 2013
oil on canvas
24 × 36 in   61 × 91 cm
after

Titian (Tiziano Vecellio)   1485–1576
Gian Giacomo Bartolotti da Parma   1518
Jacopo Sannazaro   1514–18
Pietro Aretino   1548
A Lady in White   1555
Young Man with Cap and Gloves   c.1515

RN975 **Composite Portrait after Vincent van Gogh II** 2013
oil on canvas
24 × 36 in   61 × 91 cm
after

Vincent van Gogh   1853–90
Self Portrait with Bandaged Ear   1889
Self Portrait Dedicated to Paul Gaugin   1888
Self Portrait   1887
Self Portrait with Bandaged Ear   1889

RN976 **Composite Portrait after Vincent van Gogh III** 2013
oil on canvas
24 × 36 in   61 × 91 cm
after

Vincent van Gogh   1853–90
Self Portrait with Grey Felt Hat   1887
Self Portrait with Felt Hat   1887
Self Portrait   1887
Self Portrait   1887

Memento Mori

RN965 **Memento Mori** 2013
transparency on surface mirror   framed
24 × 26 in   61 × 66 cm
edition of 12

after

after Jacques de Gheyn the Elder   1565–1629
Vanitas Still Life   1603
oil on wood
31½ × 21 in   83 × 54 cm
Metropolitan Museum of Art   New York

It's a fascinating journey to hitch a ride with Rob and Nick — never quite knowing what is around the next corner, forever altering course with intelligence and wit in their dance with light and colour that seemingly knows no bounds.

Our initial encounter was only an early staging post on this fabulous trip — the **12 Luminograms** seem to us to complete one of the early cycles of their work. Since then we have travelled with them via loosely linked inspirations of light and colour which are optimistic and uplifting, demanding of one's attention and a delight to live with.

Comprised of twelve coloured plates of graduated dense colour presented as one panelled installation Rob and Nick's **12 Luminograms** light up the space they inhabit. Each of the plates is a different colour with the intensity of enamel. The range of colour within the work blends through the installation in a simple but precise way as one colour follows another. This simplicity allows the work to continuously reconfigure and be constantly re-evaluated by its viewer. Its position in the entrance hall of a Gothic Revival 'castle' produces a tension that is an unexpected and stimulating welcome.

Michael and **Gianni Alen-Buckley**   Collectors

RN655 **12 Luminograms**   2007
Cibachrome prints mounted on aluminium and framed
12 parts   each 16 × 24 in   41 × 61 cm
edition of 12
Private collection

The Groucho Club is proud to own an entirely unique art collection that rivals many of the best in the world.

Rob and Nick Carter's work has been shown in the Club since 1999. A **Spectrum Circle** was the first of their pieces to have an instant impact.

At the Groucho we have an advantage over galleries in that there is no limit to the time an observer can spend with a piece. This, along with a convivial atmosphere, has allowed collectors to spend time with a work that otherwise would have been restricted elsewhere. This is particularly relevant with busy collectors who have been introduced to the Carters' work at the Club, notably Simon Fuller and David Walliams. **Transforming Still Life Painting** works perfectly in this context as it can be enjoyed over time, perhaps with a glass of wine, as the viewer is drawn into this ever-changing piece.

Our collection is all the richer for the privilege of having the Carters' work in it and, as well as being vital members, Nick has also acted as curator for the last 25 years, continually adding new layers of meaning to the club's wonderful collection.

Matthew Hobbs
MD   The Groucho Club   London

RN882 **Transforming Still Life Painting**   2009–12
after Ambrosius Bosschaert the Elder   **Vase with Flowers in a Window**   1618
3 hour looped film   computer   frame
23 × 28 × 5 in   58 × 71 × 13 cm
edition of 12   5 artists' proofs
Groucho Club   London

Rob and Nick Carter

Born in the UK   1968 and 1969
Rob and Nick Carter live and work in London

1987–88
Jacob Kramer School of Art and Design
1988–91
Goldsmiths College of Art   University of London
BA Hons   Fine Art and History of Art

CV

Solo Exhibitions

2013 **Transforming**
   The Fine Art Society Contemporary   London
2011 **Postcards From Vegas**
   The Cat Street Gallery   Hong Kong
   The Fine Art Society Contemporary   London
2010 **Revolve**
   The Cat Street Gallery   Hong Kong
2007 **Twelve Luminograms**
   The Fine Art Society Contemporary   London
2006 **Drawing with Light**
   Shire Hall Gallery   Staffordshire
   Painting with Light
   Bourne Fine Art   Scotland
2005 **Nouvelles Oeuvres**
   Kashya Hildebrand Gallery   Zürich
   **Painting Photographs, Light Paintings
   and Light Sculptures**
   The Fine Art Society Contemporary   London
   What Is and What Should Never Be
   a collaboration with The British Arts Council
   Said Business School   Oxford
2003 **Rob and Nick Carter**
   Mark Moore Gallery   Santa Monica   Los Angeles
   Recent Light Paintings
   Eyestorm   London
2002 **Painting with Light**
   Museum of Neon Art   Los Angeles
   Recent Work
   The Gallery in Cork Street   London
2001 **Rob and Nick Carter**
   The Market Gallery   London
2000 **Painting with Light**
   The Gallery in Cork Street   London

Group **Exhibi**tions

2013 **Vermeer, Rembrandt and Hals:**
Masterpieces of Dutch Painting from the Mauritshuis
The Frick Collection   New York
Transforming Still Life Painting
Dutch Still Life Galleries
Manchester Art Museum   Manchester
Pulse New York
The Fine Art Society Contemporary   New York
TEFAF Maastricht
The Fine Art Society Contemporary   Maastricht
Art13 London
The Fine Art Society Contemporary   London
2012 **Pulse Miami**
The Fine Art Society Contemporary   Miami
From 1820 to Now
The Fine Art Society Contemporary   Hong Kong
The British Cut
The Space   Hong Kong
Resistance: Subverting the Camera
The Fine Art Society Contemporary   London
TEFAF Maastricht
The Fine Art Society Contemporary   Maastricht
2011 **Art HK 11**
The Cat Street Gallery   Hong Kong
2010 **Harmonograph** display
in conjunction with the exhibition **Shadow Catchers**
Photography Gallery   Victoria and Albert Museum
Tondo
The Fine Art Society Contemporary   London
2007 **Luminaries and Visionaries**
Kinetica Museum   London
2004 **Into the Light**
film collaboration with Leeds band The Music
Leeds City Art Gallery   Leeds
2002 **A Colour Changing Installation**
Museum of Neon Art   Los Angeles
2001 **Some Versions of Light**
curated by Greville Worthington
The Telephone Repeater Station   Yorkshire

Public **Collec**tions

Mauritshuis   The Hague
Victoria and Albert Museum   London
Frans Hals Museum   Haarlem
Fondation Custodia / Collection Frits Lugt   Paris
Museum of Neon Art   Los Angeles
Städel Museum   Frankfurt am Main

Special **Proje**cts

2013 **Dutch Golden Age Collage**
Deckchair for The Royal Parks   London
2012 **Metropolis**
Fabergé Egg Hunt   Tower 42   City of London
2012 **Colourwash**
BT Red Phone Box for Childline   Covent Garden
2011 **Jess**
Tiger   Elephant Family Exhibition   Edinburgh
2010 **Drawing with Light Workshop**
Victoria and Albert Museum   London
Vertical Lines, Light Sculptures,
Grid Pictures, Spectrum Circle
Roof Terrace and Mildred Creak Unit
Great Ormond Street Hospital   London
2005 **MotherEarth Globe**
Christian Aid Auction   London
2002 **Absolut Carter**
Absolut Vodka for the Spirit Museum   Stockholm

Prizes and Awards

2007 Shortlisted for **The Sovereign Art Prize**
2006 Shortlisted for **The John Moores Painting Prize**

During the last fifteen years of working
together we have been fortunate enough
to be supported and inspired by a great
number of wonderful people both in
London and further afield.

There are too many to name
but you know who you are.

Thank you. We are deeply grateful.

Rob and Nick Carter   2013

Published in an edition of 2,000 copies by

The Fine Art Society Contemporary

148 New Bond Street
London W1S 2JT
+44 (0)20 7318 1895
+44 (0)20 7629 5116
contemporary@faslondon.com
www.faslondon.com

on the occasion of the exhibition

Rob and Nick Carter
Transforming
4 October – 2 November 2013

ISBN 978 1 907052 29 3

© **Rob and Nick Carter**   2013
www.robandnick.com
rob@robandnick.com

Texts © their authors as individually credited   2013

Photography
Rob and Nick Carter
except
86–89   93–94   **Patrick Burrows**
219   Tim Green
238–240   Steve Russell
225   332   Gina Soden
334   James Kelly

Printed in Italy
Print production   **Adam Shaw Associates**   Bristol

Design
Tim Barnes   ℝ   **chicken   www.herechickychicky.com**